ALSO BY NAVEEN PATNAIK

A Second Paradise: Indian Courtly Life 1590–1947

A Desert Kingdom: The Rajputs of Bikaner

The Garden of Life

The Garden *of* Life

AN INTRODUCTION TO

THE HEALING PLANTS OF INDIA

❧

Naveen Patnaik

DOUBLEDAY

New York   London   Toronto

Sydney   Auckland

PUBLISHED BY DOUBLEDAY
a division of Bantam Doubleday Dell Publishing Group, Inc.
1540 Broadway, New York, New York 10036

DOUBLEDAY and the portrayal of an anchor
with a dolphin are trademarks of Doubleday,
a division of Bantam Doubleday Dell Publishing Group, Inc.

Book design by Marysarah Quinn

Library of Congress Cataloging-in-Publication Data
Patnaik, Naveen.
The garden of life : an introduction to the healing plants of India /
Naveen Patnaik. — 1st ed.
p.   cm.
Includes bibliographical references.
1. Materia medica, Vegetable—India.   2. Medicinal plants—India.
I. Title.
RS164.P34   1993
615′.321′0954—dc20   93-18519
                                                        CIP

1   3   5   7   9   10   8   6   4   2

First Edition

Contents

III. CULINARY PLANTS

IV. COSMETIC PLANTS

V. AROMATIC PLANTS

Introduction

There is a noticeable change in the attitude of friends from other countries who visit me in India today. Once, they asked about gurus and spiritual teachers. Now they express a desire to know about Indian medicine. For a while I thought their enquiries stemmed from the general self-absorption of our times. After all, I was aware that where enlightenment had once been the rage, today physical fitness was in vogue. Then gradually I began to recognize their past interest in Indian spiritual views was not so different from their present curiosity about Indian medicine.

This realization would hardly have surprised the men who founded the Ayurveda thousands of years ago in the mountainous reaches of the Himalayas. They did not separate the external world from man's inner world, nor did they isolate man's spiritual anguish from his other sufferings.

But who were these men? The legend goes that at some time between the second and third millennium before the birth of Christ a conference was held in a Himalayan cave, attended only by the greatest sages in India. Walking thousands of miles to reach their remote destination, India's most enlightened scholars, ascetics, and teachers were drawn by the monumental purpose of their gathering. Their goal was nothing less than the alleviation of human suffering.

From their individual experience and learning these thinkers had already identified the nature of human suffering as being spiritual, mental, and physical. Now they proceeded to examine the means by which such suffering could be healed. They called their enquiries the Ayurveda, or the "Knowledge of Life."

The fundamental philosophy of Ayurveda says that suffering is disease, contentment is good health. No man is truly healthy who does not possess a sound body, a sound mind, and a sound soul. This philosophy makes Ayurveda more than a school of medicine. Its logic prescribes a whole way of life, based on knowledge and an awareness that man is interdependent with all other forms of life. Spirit is described as the intelligence of life, matter as its energy. Both are manifestations of the principle of Brahman, the one-ness of life.

To the founders of Ayurveda, mankind's goal was the understanding of this principle. The man who recognizes how he is linked with universal life is a man who possesses a sound soul because he is not isolated from his own energies, nor from the energies of nature. But as the highest form of life, man also becomes its guardian, recognizing his very survival depends on seeing that the fragile balance of nature, and living organisms, is not disturbed.

In Ayurvedic terms, this means that man must prevent wanton destruction. What he takes he must replace, to preserve the equilibrium of nature. If he cuts down a tree for his own uses, he must plant another. He must ensure the purity of water. He must not poison the air. He must not poison the soil. Ayurveda, some four thousand years ago, was already propagating the arguments which inform the ecological debate of our own time.

The logic of Ayurvedic philosophy, with its insistence on maintaining nature's equilibrium, continues by observing that if a man's spiritual health is dependent on his ability to live in harmony with the external universe, his mental health must depend on his ability to live in harmony with himself.

From its very origins this science paid as much attention to the illnesses of the mind as to illnesses of the body. A separate school of Ayurvedic medicine developed to administer to the diseases of the mind. Its physicians identified the techniques of deep breathing and meditation for quieting the mind and for improving the memory and other mental capacities, that practitioners of yoga would later use. Sedatives and tranquilizers were known and used by early Ayurvedic physicians. To calm the mind, and reinforce its own balance, Ayurveda noted the ways in which aromatics, diet, even cosmetics could help sustain mental equilibrium.

But again, because the originators of the Ayurveda saw every illness and every form of health as part of an interlocking whole, a man's mental condition was seen as having both a physical and a social impact. The morally ill man was also the mentally ill man. If a man willfully disturbed the balance of living things he inevitably damaged himself. The Ayurvedic doctor tried to make his patient understand that in order to avoid suffering, the patient must control his own destructive and self-destructive instincts.

Finally, there is Ayurveda's concern with physiological suffering. The three great sages of Ayurveda, the men known as the triad of its knowledge, all emphasized the importance of preventive medicine. Their goal was to develop an individual's own immune system to such a degree that the body became its own best medicine, fighting off infection before disease could take serious hold. They also understood that many diseases were beyond a patient's mental or physical control. These diseases they identified in as much detail as possible, and then searched for their cures.

The first great Ayurvedic teacher, Agnivesh, was a disciple of Atreya Punavarsu, one of that original body of thinkers who founded the Ayurveda. Instructed by the sage to commit to memory the observations and knowledge exchanged at the conference, this master of Ayurvedic science, who is also thought to have trained the Buddha's personal physician, described the body as made up of minute particles invisible to the human eye, each particle carrying its own inherited and individual information. Without the aid of microscopes Agnivesh was already intuiting molecular biology and genetic coding. The sophistication of Ayurveda's original insights meant that from the very beginning its physicians conducted their diagnoses by studying muscle structure; blood and circulation; bone; bone marrow; the vital organs of the heart, the lungs, and the liver; generative tissue under which they identified both the sperm and the ovum; and the three human wastes, namely, sweat, urine, and excretia.

The sages of the Ayurveda were aware of the medicinal plants known and used by the so-called aboriginal Indian tribes who had inhabited India's forests from the beginning of history. So the second task they set themselves was the collation and examination of this medical information into what we would call today the first Indian medical and botanical encyclopedia.

Staggeringly, this growing mass of knowledge, constantly expanded by successive Ayurvedic physicians, was committed to memory and handed down orally from teacher to student for over a thousand years before it was finally written down in the first century A.D. by Ayurveda's third legendary physician, Charaka.

By Charaka's time Ayurvedic science had already developed into eight specialized schools of medicine. Long before the birth of Christ, and millennia before the birth of European medicine, Ayurveda had specialists in the following fields: Psychiatry; Pediatrics; Gynecology; Ear, Nose, and Throat; Ophthalmology; Surgery; Toxicology; Virility and Fertility.

Perhaps the most interesting aspect of ancient Ayurveda to the modern mind is the sheer extent of medical possibilities searched for by an Ayurvedic physician all those centuries ago before he made a diagnosis. This same exhaustive and lengthy procedure is followed by the Ayurvedic physician of today.

According to Charaka's treatise, in order to treat a patient a doctor must first have an exhaustive theoretical knowledge of the nature of all known diseases, since preliminary symptoms are often the same whether a disease is mild or severe. Then through detailed discussion and his own trained observations the physician should examine the patient. A patient's personal history and background are considered of great significance since residents of different regions are accustomed to differing diets, habits, and climates, and show a variety of mental inclinations. Then the doctor should conduct an investigation of the patient's internal sounds, respiratory and intestinal. This should be followed by investigating circulation through the taking of the pulse and temperature. Charaka emphasizes that the malfunctioning of the digestive process is the first symptom of all diseases. The physician should also gather all possible information about a patient's digestion, bowel and urinary movements. If the physician deems it necessary, he should conduct analyses of the patient's blood, stool, and urine.

Now the physician must test the patient's mental clarity, by assessing his (or her) memory and acuteness of sensory perceptions. He must enquire after the patient's dreams, aversions, fears, desires, and any irregularities of behavior. He must try and ascertain the patient's emotional state. He must judge the patient's capacity for physical exercise, his vitality, and his mental and physical equilibrium. Only after a physician has done all this does Ayurveda deem a physician's diagnosis to be complete.

With the predominance of Western medicine in the world today, we are all familiar with Hippocrates and the code this great Greek physician believed should govern the behavior of a physician. But the *Treatise of Charaka* also describes a code, one that had been in operation for the physicians of Ayurveda more than a thousand years before it was ever written down.

According to Charaka, an Ayurvedic physician must observe the absolute privacy of his patient. He may not divulge any information about his patient or the patient's household, not even the patient's address. He is forbidden from deserting his patient under any circumstances, no matter how serious or how infectious the disease. A physician must be open to new medical and diagnostic information, remaining a student of medicine all his life for the continuing benefit of his patients. To achieve this end, Ayurveda lays great stress on periodic discussion and debate with other physicians either at conferences or in private dialogue.

Theoretical knowledge, clarity of reasoning, wide practical experience, and personal skill are described as the four valued qualifications of the Ayurvedic physician. He must also lead a disciplined life, be gentle and compassionate, and exhibit unswerving devotion to his professional duties.

Charaka's treatise lays down an exact code governing the training of a physician. The student must live an austere life during his studies, devoting all his time and energies to the acquisition of knowledge. Although most Ayurvedic medicines are from plant sources, the remainder come from mineral and animal products often used in combination with plants to make medicine, which means the Ayurvedic student needs a wide knowledge of chemistry and botany, as well as biology. Finally, he has to be sufficiently educated in philosophy to be capable of preparing a terminally ill patient to face death.

A student who desires to practice Ayurvedic science may choose his own teacher and his own branch of Ayurvedic science, but once that choice is made, and once he is accepted by a teacher, the disciple must live in his teacher's household as an obedient son, following a rigid schedule until the teacher considers his education complete.

Because the knowledge of Ayurveda was thought to be beyond price, a student's medical instruction was given free of charge by his professor, who repeatedly impressed upon the student his obligations to his future patients and to society in general. After the student had become a physician himself, it was considered acceptable to aspire to wealth, recognition, and fame. Other-worldliness was not required, only that when the time came, he was to impart his knowledge of medicine to his own students, free of charge.

A qualified Ayurvedic physician was expected to maintain his own dispensary and nursing home, hiring attendants and nurses to run them at the highest level of hygiene. Most importantly, he had to be able to prepare his own medicines from raw materials.

Ayurveda still insists that a physician know what is in the medicine he prescribes to a patient. As Charaka says in a scathing observation as relevant to the medicine of today as it was twenty centuries ago, "A physician without knowledge of pharmacoepia, a scholar without knowledge of grammar, and an archer without practice—all three are laughed at as fools."

Even today, with all the additional information available as a result of the huge expansion of world medical knowledge, Ayurveda pays homage to its original founders. Three quarters of its medicines are still plant based, and contemporary physicians find these medicinal plants seem to create far fewer side effects than the chemically produced medicines prescribed by Western medicine.

The goal of this science which calls itself the Knowledge of Life is rejuvenation. Not the pursuit of lost youth, but the maintaining of a man in his prime, whatever his age, both in his mental and in his physical capacity, because only then can a human being aspire to the greatest of human goals—the consciousness of his connection with the principle of life, the awareness of the Brahman.

Such consciousness requires an appreciation of all life—that which precedes an individual and that which follows him. And in this great task, the Ayurvedic physician draws on Indian civilization's ancient veneration and study of plants.

India's oldest known body of wisdom lies in the hymns of the Rig-Veda. Perhaps it is no accident that many of these were thought to have been written by Agnivesh's guru, one of the original sages of the Ayurveda.

If any hymn were to be ascribed to this great thinker, then it must surely be the first prayer of the Indian physician:

You herbs, born at the birth of time
More ancient than the gods themselves.
O Plants, with this hymn I sing to you
Our mothers and our gods.

The holy fig tree is your home.
A thousand are your growths.
You, who have a thousand powers,
Free this my patient from disease.

Fly, Spirit of Disease.
Be gone with the bluejay and the kingfisher.
Fly with the wind's impetuous speed.
Vanish together with the storm.

Most excellent of all are you, O Plants.
Your vassals are the trees.
Let him be subject to your powers
The man who seeks to injure You.

When restoring vanished strength
I hold you herbs within my hand.
And the Spirit of Disease departs,
Cheated of another death.

Reliever is your mother's name.
Hence, restorers are you called.
Rivers are you, with wings that fly.
Keep distant that which brings disease.

Unharmed be he who digs you up.
Unharmed the man for whom I dig.
And let no malady destroy
The lives within your guardianship.

Hymn in Praise of Herbs, Rig-Veda (circa 2500 B.C.)

History
of the
Ayurveda

*I*ndians believe that the knowledge of medicinal plants is older than history itself, gifted hundreds of thousands of years ago to the original inhabitants of India by Brahma, the Divine Creator. Thus, when the sages of the Ayurveda sought to heal human suffering they were able to draw on a knowledge that had already been evolving for millennia in the forests of India.

The triad of Ayurveda's legendary physicians are considered to have been Atreya Punavarsu, one of the sages present at the original conference. The second is his disciple, Agnivesh, who collated all the thinking and knowledge exchanged at that gathering, to form the science of Ayurveda. This core of knowledge, continually expanding and improving, was then handed down orally for nearly two thousand years until the third member of Ayurveda's venerated triad, Charaka, provided Indian medicine with its first written text in the *Charaka Samhita* or *Treatise of Charaka*.

Long before Charaka's appearance, the study and use of medicinal plants in Ayurvedic medicine had already spread throughout India with such force that by the third century B.C. the Emperor Asoka, whose empire covered most of the Indian subcontinent, was providing what we would call today free health care to all his subjects.

Asoka established free hospitals, hospices, and dispensaries as well as veterinary centers throughout his vast empire. Patients could make voluntary contributions to these establishments, but no one was asked for payment to be cured of ill health. The state maintained the forests which provided so many of the plants used in Ayurvedic medicine, and established its own botanical and herbal gardens for the cultivation of medicinal herbs. The destruction of forests and the pollution of water was banned by imperial edicts carved on rock, which can be seen in Indian museums today and which continue to astonish the contemporary mind with their extraordinary and compassionate vision.

But it was in the time of the Emperor Asoka's grandfather that the first European records of Indian medicinal plants were begun, by the physicians and generals who accompanied Alexander the Great on his campaigns in India. It is thought that the international exchange of information on India's plant medicine predates both Alexander and Ayurveda, since indigenous Indian seeds such as coriander have been found in the tombs of the Egyptian pharaohs, and Indian plants were used by the textile makers of Mesopotamia for the making of dyes. This means that Indian plants were being traded to other countries at the time of India's ancient Indus Valley civilization, which existed around 3000 B.C. Meanwhile travelers were taking this same information overland through Tibet into China, suggesting that over five thousand years ago knowledge of India's plant pharmacopoeia was being exchanged throughout the known civilized world.

The second great impetus to international knowledge of Indian plant medicine was provided by Arab traders, centuries before the birth of Islam. The Queen of Sheba traded the spices of India to the Israelites, at the time of King Solomon. For the next fifteen hundred years the merchants of Asia Minor held a monopoly of western trade in Indian plants and spices. Ayurvedic science began to be studied by Arab physicians and Indian medical plants entered the Arab Materia Medica, whose physicians imparted this information to the Greeks and Romans. So widespread was such knowledge that by the first century A.D. when Charaka was creating Ayurveda's first written treatise, Pliny was already describing the plants of India to the Roman Empire in his *Natural History*.

Charaka's treatise describes 1,500 plants and identifies 350 of them as valuable for medicinal purposes. But as a physician Charaka's interest lay in diagnosis and prescription. Ayurvedic surgery had to wait four hundred years before the great Ayurvedic surgeon Susruta described the methods of Indian surgery in the *Treatise of Susruta*, written around A.D. 400, detailing the performance of an operation for peritonitis, and even such exact operations as those required for the cranium, ear, nose, and throat.

For the next millennium Ayurvedic texts were added to by many other physicians and surgeons, and Arab traders conveyed this information to the physicians of the Arab, Greek, and Roman worlds, whose own knowledge would eventually form the basis of European medicine. Although the medicine practiced by the physicians of the Moorish Empire in Spain was far in advance of the primitive medical knowledge of medieval Europe, and Europeans were learning medical science through the writings of later

Arabs such as the great Avicenna of Bukhara or the physician and philosopher Averroës of Cordoba, Europeans had begun to grasp the value of India's medicinal plants and spices.

By the fifteenth century, having expelled the Arabs from Spain, European powers now sought to break the Arab monopoly on the trade of Indian spices and medicines, and find their own routes to India. At this moment of history India's vast knowledge of plant pharmacopoeia launched fleet after European fleet—British, French, Dutch, Spanish, Portuguese. Isabella and Ferdinand, the rulers of Spain, financed an expedition by Columbus, and it might be said that Ayurveda led to the discovery of America, since Columbus's mission was to find new access to the spices of India—those fabled spices which could preserve foods, provide aromatics and cosmetics, and produce medicines.

While Europe was searching for means to acquire India's spices and plants, Ayurvedic medicine was flourishing in India, absorbing into its own medical knowledge the information produced by Graeco-Arab medicine. The Moghul Empire was at its zenith in the India of this time. The records of successive emperors give evidence of the robustness of Ayurvedic medicine. Further evidence of this flowering is provided by a succession of Europeans who traveled to India in the fifteenth, sixteenth, and seventeenth centuries.

It was Ayurveda's tragedy that India began to fragment with the decay of the Moghul Empire at the end of the seventeenth century. As India disintegrated into civil war, the great centers of Indian learning fell apart, and scholarship was dispersed by two centuries of political unrest. Ayurvedic knowledge retreated into the villages, temples, and small courts of India, where sometimes in the hands of demagogic kings and priests, a great science was reduced to primitive ritual.

During this period the power of Europe was rising, and by the middle of the nineteenth century, the British, flush with the progressive thinking of the Industrial Revolution, established their empire in India. The study of Ayurveda was by now so diminished that the British dismissed it as nothing more than an additional native superstition which it was the white man's burden to remove.

For a whole century of British rule Indians colluded with Western thought in despising Indian scientific learning, until the turn of our own century produced the latest turn in Ayurveda's fortunes. Fired by a new nationalism, patriotic Indian physicians trained in Western medicine, as well as enlightened Englishmen, began to examine the claims made by Ayurvedic medicine. The small Ayurvedic centers began to flourish again. New ones were established as the power of plant medicine and the depth of Ayurveda's plant pharmacopoeia was understood. But it was not until India became independent that Ayurveda began to regain a reputation as a valid school of medicine.

The Indian government has now opened laboratories for the clinical testing of Ayurveda's medical plants. Indian forest departments are studying and growing these plants in scientific conditions, advised by the forest dwellers whose ancestors cultivated forest plants for countless millennia. The country's botanical gardens are creating and preserving Indian herbaria, so that Ayurvedic physicians have a constant source of medicinal plants. And more and more people, Indians and visitors from the West, are now visiting Ayurvedic centers.

What would a visitor to a reputable Ayurvedic center find today? The finest Ayurvedic centers are currently in south India. These centers believe their treatments are unique, based as they are on the *Panch Karma*, or the Five Therapies of detoxifying the body, which Ayurveda holds essential for the regeneration of the body's tissues, muscles, and bones, even if a patient does not have an obvious medical illness. Therefore, a series of emetics, purges, enemas, and nasal baths made from prominent Ayurvedic plant extracts are the first step of the treatment. This cleansing process is then followed by inducing sweating in steam and dry baths. When the poisons which can be released through the skin are removed, the body is then massaged over a period of days with different medicinal oils. The south Indian centers subscribe to the traditional Ayurvedic philosophy which holds that the human body must go through this process of detoxification at least once a year to rejuvenate itself, and consider their treatments particularly effective for nervous and neurological problems.

Many other diseases are also treated in modern Ayurvedic centers, and the physicians cultivate their own gardens of medicinal plants, as well as acquiring herbs from forest dwellers who collect them in the wild. The patient is fed on a diet in which purity is of particular significance, so the center maintains its own dairy and beehives, as well as its own vegetable gardens.

Ayurvedic centers have their own laboratories where the plants and their mixtures are compounded according to exact prescriptions. Because this school of medicine is a high science, from its very inception Ayurveda has warned people against quack practitioners or from attempting to formulate its medicines themselves. Today Ayurvedic surgery is not practiced, in deference to the great advances made in surgical methods by Western medicine, but its plant medicines are gaining in reputation all the time. Clinical tests are being conducted which often confirm the claims made by Ayurvedic medicine.

Apart from medical centers, Ayurvedic medicine is rapidly becoming commercialized in India, and certain plant medicines are being produced with modern technology in the forms of pills, oils, and mixtures, which appear to be finding increasing acceptance, both in India and abroad.

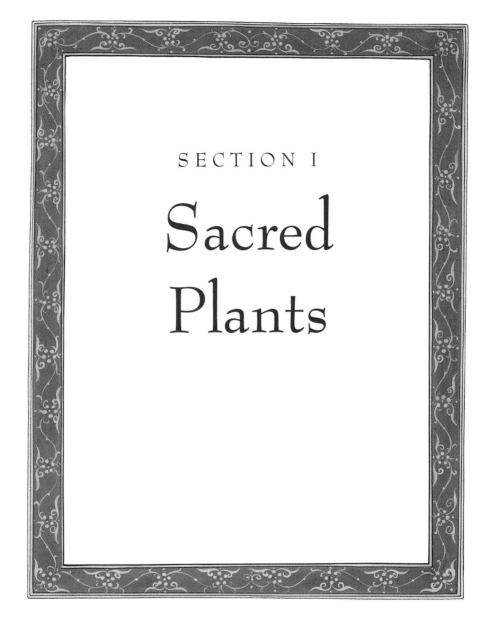

SECTION I

Sacred
Plants

SACRED PLANTS

*A*rchaeological evidence shows the earliest inhabitants of the Indian subcontinent held plants in great reverence. But nature worship among primitive peoples is not unusual. What makes the Indian reverence for plants unique is its unbroken continuity from prehistory to the present day, when plants have long since ceased to be the major source of human food, clothing, and shelter.

Every Indian attitude toward plants, from prehistoric to modern times, is still visible in India today.

As early as 3000 B.C. the prehistoric worship of actual plants was already turning into a reverence for nature as a source of medicine. Seals found in India's earliest cities of the Indus Valley civilization show plants were regarded less as holy in themselves than as the home of divine spirits with powers beneficial to mankind.

By the time Ayurveda became a serious science, these beneficial powers had long been acknowledged in the vast medicinal pharmacopoeia contained in plants. What primitive peoples worshipped as a plant's magical powers was now analyzed by the Ayurvedic physicians for its physical powers.

The scientific approach may have dispelled superstition, but it certainly did not diminish a plant's sacredness in the eyes of the Ayurvedic physician to whom knowledge was sacred, as it was to all Indian thinkers. Indeed, the great Indian philosophers conducted their dialogues in the forest using plants again and again to illustrate concepts of spiritual continuity to their students, because the forest represented the endless self-regeneration of life, or what we would call today an ecosystem, complete in itself.

Even kings yearned to be free of their material responsibilities to pursue the higher enlightenment provided by plants, as shown in the seventh-century novel, written by Bānabhatta, *Kadambari*:

He gave up his usual pleasures for the joys of the forest. Trees were now his palaces; creepers, his harem; fawns, his friends; bark garments his regal robes; prayer beads now his weapons; and his treasury, prayer.

In contemporary India offerings left at the base of trees indicate that plants are still worshipped as they once were, especially by the tribal populations who are the descendants of India's oldest inhabitants, her forest dwellers.

The vast pantheon of Indian divinities are still offered plants in rituals which hold certain plants holy to certain gods, as prescribed by Hinduism's earliest priests.

Indian philosophy continues to use nature's completeness as a philosophical metaphor, whether it is in the lotus sermon of the Buddha or the enlightenment to be acquired from meditating under a tree.

And Ayurvedic physicians continue to examine the scientific basis for a plant's reputation as holy, to see if new medicines can be found.

1
Banyan

(*Ficus bengalensis*)
Family: Moraceae
Sanskrit name: Nyagrodha
Hindi name: Bar

There is in India a tree whose property it is to plant itself. It spreads out mighty arms to the earth, where in the space of a single year the arms take root and put forth anew.

Pliny (A.D. 70)

＊

Called "The Many-Footed" after the aerial roots striding from its trunk to form a small forest, the canopy of a single banyan tree has been known to extend two thousand feet.

Three thousand years before Pliny described it to the Roman Empire this mighty shade tree struck awe in the Aryan nomads sweeping across India. Their priests likened the banyan's outpouring of vitality to a flow of light or to a liquid immortality overflowing onto the earth from the goblets of the gods themselves. Their chiefs drank ritually of its sap, believing it could increase their virility and ensure their hold upon conquered lands.

Over the centuries, as the actual properties of the tree were examined for their medicinal value, it was discovered that an infusion of banyan seeds did indeed make a tonic sufficiently invigorating to be widely regarded as an aphrodisiac, while banyan latex applied externally accelerated the healing of wounds and open sores.

Ayurvedic doctors also noted that medicines derived from the banyan assisted in blood clotting, contained major antiseptic and astringent properties, and an infusion from banyan bark alleviated diabetes.

The extreme longevity of "The Many-Footed" seemed to support claims for its immortality. For instance, two banyans, at Prayag and Gaya, described as already ancient by scribes writing in 400 B.C., lived long enough to be admired in the seventeenth century by Emperor Jahāngīr, to whom King James I sent an ambassador to establish Britain's first trade links with India.

The British traders who followed King James's ambassador observed that Indian merchants, or *banias*, frequently conducted their business under this great tree, considering a contract made in its shade to be binding. Sometimes as many as a thousand *banias* collected between the plunging roots of one tree as if it were a stock exchange made of living wood, leading the British to name the tree of the *banias* the banyan.

The banyan is still used as an assembly hall in rural India, not just by merchants, but by village elders in council or by priests celebrating religious occasions; it is the shaded piazza where men and women gather for discussions in the evenings and where school-children are taught by day, and where farmers herd their animals to escape the searing summer sun. Remedies from the tree are still used by India's villagers, raised to know its healing properties, and by Ayurvedic doctors preparing medicines for their patients in the cities.

Is it any wonder that this life-giving and life-preserving tree, capable as Pliny said, of planting itself, should have been revered by the earliest philosopher-sages of India? Or that they should have enjoined mankind to contemplate the banyan's secret sacredness?

He,
the Powerful
and the Holy
holds straight this tree
in unsupported space.
       Its rays,
       whose roots
       are high above,
       stream downward.
Deep
may they sink
within us,
and be
Hidden.

    Invocation from the Rig-Veda
    (circa 2500 B.C.)

2
Lotus

(*Nelumbo nucifera*)
Family: Nelumbonaceae
Sanskrit name: Padma
Hindi name: Kamal

In the beginning were the waters. Matter readied itself. The sun glowed. And a lotus slowly opened, holding the universe on its golden pericarp.

Indian creation myth

❈

To the Indian imagination this beautiful water flower is associated with divinity. An early medieval Hindu text describes a goddess as being,

> Slender as a lotus-fiber,
> Lotus-eyed,
> In the lotus posture,
> Pollen dusting her lotus-feet,
> She dwells
> In the pendant lotus of the heart.

More significantly, the lotus is a symbol of enlightenment. Soaring toward the sun, untainted by the clay water in which it grows, the lotus is used by Indian philosophers as an exemplar of the soul—an illustration of the doorway that opens backward into the waters of birth, or forward into revelation.

The lotus is central to the practitioners of *kundalini* yoga who believe the *kundalini*, or potent occult energy, that lies coiled in man like a sleeping serpent can be awakened through yogic disciplines and meditations. Once aroused, this serpent of wisdom ascends "fine as a lotus-fiber" through a succession of psychic centers described as "lotus-chakras," until it reaches the last and highest chakra which opens as "the thousand-petaled lotus of understanding," revealing the brightness of the Self like a universal flame no wind has ever disturbed.

Appropriately, the medicinal properties of the lotus appear to aid concentration and Ayurvedic science extracts medicines from the lotus, which are antiallergenic, antispasmodic, and astringent. The beauty of the lotus is also considered a medicine.

3
Holy Basil

(*Ocimum sanctum*)
Family: Labiatae
Sanskrit name: Tulasi
Hindi name: Tulasi

Almost all the Hindus . . . adore a plant like our Basilico gentile, *but of more pungent odor. Every one before his house has a little altar . . . in the middle of which they erect certain pedestals like little towers, and in these the shrub is grown.*

P. Vincenzo Maria, A Voyage to India (1672)

Modern science has established that this modest aromatic shrub perceptibly purifies the air within a wide radius of its vicinity, proving most effective just before sunrise, the time when it is ritually circled by the devout.

Perhaps this is why Hindu myths say the King of Death himself gives way before this holy shrub, and why each year, at the waxing of the autumn moon, the plant is married in a religious ritual to one of the three gods of the Hindu trinity, Vishnu the Preserver.

Any domestic courtyard which is centered around the holy basil is considered in India a place of peace, piety, and virtue.

The plant's roots symbolize religious pilgrimage, its branches divinity, its crown an understanding of the scriptures. Traditionally, once the shrub has been planted in an Indian courtyard it is nurtured for three months before it is worshipped with offerings of rice, flowers, and lighted lamps. After that, virgins pray to the holy basil for husbands, married women for domestic peace and prosperity.

Medically, the plant provides a pharmacopoeia for the entire household. Its leaves are crushed in honey and used to cure coughs, colds, and bronchitis, and to reduce fevers. An infusion of basil leaves and ginger is India's most popular remedy for stomachaches in children. Its essential oil is an antiseptic and insect repellent, while its root, reduced to paste, soothes bites and stings, acting even as an antidote to snake venom and scorpion bites.

4
Flame-of-the-Forest

(*Butea monosperma*)
Family: Papilionaceae
Sanskrit name: Palasha
Hindi name: Dhak

Curved like crescent moons,
the crimson petals glowed in the forest lands
Like nail-marks from Spring's passionate
embrace.
Kalidasa, *The Birth of Kumara* (circa A.D. 400)

The flame-of-the-forest is among India's most venerated trees, with its colorful flowers. Indeed, in ceremonies which honor other trees or which inaugurate the planting of trees, the twigs of the flame-of-the-forest are rubbed together to ignite a sacrificial flame.

At the ceremony marking a Hindu priest's son's symbolic entrance into manhood, the youth is given a staff made from the flame-of-the-forest, and at the end of life, it is a log made from this sacred wood which is used to light a Hindu's funeral pyre.

According to the *Charaka Samhita*, the tree's seeds are insecticidal and Ayurvedic physicians use them to compound medicines for diarrhea and dysentery. Juice made from the tree's roots, bark, and leaves are administered for regulating menstrual flow, and in stomach ailments such as colic and intestinal worms, while an ointment made from the leaves is useful for boils, pimples, swellings, and for shrinking hemorrhoids.

During the spring festival of Holi, young men smear a powder made from dried petals of the flame-of-the-forest flower onto the faces of passing young women, the brilliant red color carrying an obvious erotic message.

But the flowers are also used to obtain the red dye in which Buddhist monks color their robes. They wear the flamelike color as a symbol of renunciation, signifying the fire which burns away all desire.

5
Coconut

(*Cocos nucifera*)
Family: Palmaceae
Sanskrit name: Narikela
Hindi name: Nariyal

He who sees a straight coconut palm will go direct to heaven.

Traditional Indian saying

The strong winds buffeting the coasts where the graceful coconut palm grows make it almost impossible to find a straight coconut tree, so Indians ensure an additional path to heaven by offering its large, oval nut in their religious rituals.

Fishermen offer coconuts to the sea to propitiate Varuna, Lord of Winds and Waters. The coconut is an essential element in wedding ceremonies, often placed in a pot which is a metaphor for the womb, while the nut itself, a symbol of life, confers fertility on the bridal couple. In parts of southern India coconuts are preserved as images of ancestors, occupying a prominent place on family altars.

The extreme antiquity of the use of coconuts in Indian religious rites is reflected in the "black" rituals still practiced by arcane cults, who, unable any longer to sacrifice human skulls to their bloodthirsty gods, offer instead the coconut, so similar in size and shape to a man's head.

The coconut is considered by Indians to be the fruit of aspiration, and a guarantee of auspicious beginnings: a coconut is split at the inauguration of any Indian function, from the launching of a ship to the first take of a movie spectacular, to invite the blessings of the gods.

But the true sacredness of the coconut comes from the spectrum of food and medicine it offers for the use of mankind. High in proteins, minerals, and vitamins, and representing an ecosystem complete in itself, the coconut provides milk, water, cream, oil, and hard flesh to Ayurvedic medicine for a variety of cures, from the treatment of burns and the restoration of hair growth, to the dissolving of kidney stones and treatments for the heart and blood pressure.

6
Bel

(*Aegle marmelos*)
Family: Rutaceae
Sanskrit name: Bilva
Hindi name: Bel

❖

The great night of Siva is the most sacred time for fasts, prayers, and offerings, when even the most involuntary acts, if pleasing to Siva, are made holy.

There was a poor hunter once, who happened to take shelter during the night in Siva's sacred Bel tree.

He was delivered from the encumbrance of all previous existences.

The Siva Purana (seventh century A.D.)

The Bel is unmistakably Siva's tree: tall, stern, austere, with dark leaves and fruit like pale suns. The trifoliate leaves symbolize the three eyes of Siva, and are known to contain a small percentage of Siva's alchemical substance, mercury. It is said that offerings of water sprinkled on these leaves at any shrine will always remain fresh.

In the Atharva-Veda (circa 1000 B.C.) the Bel is described as being so sacred its timber may not be burned as fuel. Today the tree is still the totemic deity of those great guardians of eastern Indian forests, the Santhal tribals.

The scientists of the Ayurveda value the Bel tree for the medicinal properties contained in its fruit and leaves. A decoction of leaves is a favorite remedy for ailments that often occur during seasonal changes—fevers, influenza, fatigue. The fruit has a hard rind or shell that cracks open to reveal a pale tawny flesh, which is astringent and very sweet. Pulped, the flesh of the Bel is an excellent curative for dysentery, while the fragrant juice is used as an appetizer, for curing stomach disorders, and for purifying the blood.

Both sustaining as food and curative as medicine, Bels are traditionally called by Indians the "fruit of plenty," so perhaps it is no irony that Puranic legends should describe the fruit of Siva's austere tree as the breasts of the Goddess of Plenty.

7
Ustram Bead

(*Elaeocarpus ganitrus*)
Family: Elaeocarpaceae
Sanskrit name: Rudraksha
Hindi name: Rudraksha

The Lord of the Universe drew his bow and unleashed his arrows at the triple city, burning its demons and hurling them into the western ocean, for the welfare of creation.
  Then the Three-Eyed God restrained the fire born of his own anger, saying to it: "Enough! Do not reduce the world to ash!"
  The Mahabharata (circa 300 B.C.)

The ustram bead tree gains its Western name from its fruit, hard kernels which are dried and strung into rosaries by followers of that most awesome god of the Hindu trinity, Siva the Destroyer.

Ustram bead necklaces are also treasured by other Indians, who wear them to regulate the blood pressure and to tranquilize the mind against nervous disorders.

When dried, the ustram bead is about the size of a marble with brainlike configurations which are commonly referred to as its "faces." Worth its own weight in gold, a bead's value is determined not only by its size but by the number of faces with which Nature has endowed it, from the rare single-faced bead representing the One Reality treasured by temples, through twenty-one faces symbolic of various philosophical concepts, to the fused or double bead symbolizing infinity, which is set in gold, emerald, and rubies.

The ascetic followers of Siva have given the bead his name, the rudraksha. Rudra is another name for Siva, and his devotees believe the rudraksha bead is the tear of rage which fell from Rudra's eye as he beheld the effrontery of mankind.

Legend says the Destroyer wept when he witnessed the towering metropolis or "triple city" created by man's superbly ambitious technology. In its arrogance, this magnificent human creation had undermined the balance between the earth, the atmosphere, and the sky.

Then, according to *The Mahabharata*, having shed the implacable tear which turned into an ustram bead, "The Lord of the Universe . . . unleashed his arrows at the triple city . . . for the welfare of creation."

8
Indian Hemp

(*Cannabis sativa*)
Family: Cannabinaceae
Sanskrit name: Vijaya
Hindi name: Bhang

Banged up to the eyes.
British colonial description of celebrants
using Indian hemp or cannabis

Honored by Indians as one of the "Precious Things" recovered at the birth of the universe from the primeval sea, Indian hemp or cannabis, as this narcotic plant is more popularly known, was taken by the king of the gods to gain immortality. In Sanskrit the plant is called *Vijaya* or Conquest, because it is supposed to have granted victory to those gods who used it.

In time, a cannabis potion known as bhang became the accepted pleasure drink of Siva, Lord of Wandering Ascetics. Indeed, an affectionate folk name for Siva in this mode is *Bhangeri Baba* or "bhang-exhilarated Father." During the medieval period, bhang entered the temple, taken by temple celebrants as a ritual drink to reach religious ecstasy. As a ceremonial sherbet it entered the pleasures of the court. Ground very fine, hemp was sifted through muslin that had been refolded up to six times. Then it was blended into thickened milk and seasoned with crushed almonds, lotus seeds, black peppers, aromatic herbs, and cane syrup.

Bhang was also widely used by the general populace during the spring celebrations of the Holi festival, which followed the winter harvest, when feuds and social classifications were joyfully dissolved in uninhibited gaiety.

At first a stimulant, exhilarant, and aphrodisiac, thereafter a sedative, the active principle of Indian hemp lies in the plant resin. Forty percent of this principle was used in the resinous hashish smoked by the wandering sects of India; 26 percent in the dried flower heads smoked in the villages of India as "ganja"; and only 10 percent in the ground green leaves used for the preparation of the bhang drink.

Ayurvedic medicine used hemp for the alleviation of migraine headaches and stomach spasms. Today it is still valued for its beneficent effect on migraines and neuralgia. A recognized analgesic, hemp is an antispasmodic and an anodyne or pain soother. It is also known to promote digestion and to assist in the flow of urine.

The plant's widespread medical, religious, and recreational uses in India were noted by a sixteenth-century Dutch botanist, Iohn van Lincschoten, in *His Discours of Voyages into Ye Easte and Weste Indies* (1598): "They have many kinds of Drogues, such as Amfira or Opium, Camfora, *Bangue*, and Sandall Wood."

9
Sacred Fig

(*Ficus religiosa*)
Family: Moraceae
Sanskrit name: Ashvattha
Hindi name: Pipal

Among trees I am the Ashvattha.
Krishna, *The Bhagavad-Gita*
(200 B.C.–A.D. 200)

＊

*L*ord Krishna's metaphor in the holy book of the Hindus is easily understood by Indians who believe the wood of the *Asvattha* or sacred fig was used to light the original sacred fire with which the gods granted knowledge to the human race.

India honors the sacred fig as the Tree of Life. The earliest evidence of this reverence was discovered by archaelogists excavating the five-thousand-year-old remains of the Indus Valley civilization, when they found seals already depicting the sacred fig circled by worshippers. Today, believers still sit under the sacred fig, meditating on the Creator.

In ancient India the constant whisper of leaves on the sacred fig's elongated leaf stems was likened to the hum of India's oldest musical instrument, the vina or lute, and the planting of fig trees was both an act of merit and a means of ratifying peace treaties. As befits the tree of life, its medical properties were found to contribute to the health of the vital functions—circulation, vision, the lungs, and the kidneys.

So deeply is this tree associated with both the origin and the symbiosis of life that it is thought to induce illumination, and countless Indian legends tell of sages meditating in its shade. The greatest of them came to be known as Enlightened One or the Buddha, and his tree the Bodhi, or Tree of Enlightenment. Buddhists often depict the Buddha in the shape of this tree, which has become the Buddhist symbol of consciousness.

In 288 B.C. the Indian emperor Asoka gifted a graft of the tree under which the Buddha had meditated, to the king of Sri Lanka. Today that grafted tree is still circled by chanting devotees.

When the original Bodhi tree withered in India, a graft from the Sri Lankan tree was planted in its place, where it continues to provide a living link between the Buddha and those who seek enlightenment.

10

Jamun

(*Syzygium cumini*)
Family: Myrtaceae
Sanskrit name: Jambu
Hindi name: Jamun

In the Continent of the Jamun Trees, where
the land of India lies . . .

Indian ritual invocation

⁂

The ripening fruit of the jamun tree signals the approach of summer, a time when children and parakeets battle over its heavy purple berries and every mouth is stained with juice.

Old men with long staves patiently knock the berries onto cloths spread on the ground. Beneath the flesh of the berries lie pits, which are crushed into flour for treating diabetes. The juice itself is an excellent liver stimulant, while decoctions from the bark are used to cure mouth ulcers and for strengthening the gums. The powdered bark is commonly used as a tooth powder.

A generous plant that fruits abundantly, the jamun is described in *The Mahabharata* as a cosmic tree standing to the south of Mount Meru, the axis of the universe. When the ripened fruit of this gigantic tree burst, its juice fell in waterfalls, making a river which becomes the boundaries of a land known as *Jambu-dvipa*, or the Continent of the Jamun Trees, populated by epic heroes who gained immortality by drinking the juice.

What probably began as a boastful traveler's tale or nomadic road directions became somehow the name by which ancient Indians identified their location in a mythic space and time, so although the jamun tree receives no ostensible worship, it is still invoked at formal Indian rituals, which always commence with the words: "In the Continent of the Jamun Trees, where the land of India lies . . ."

11
Margosa

(*Azadirachta indica*)
Family: Meliaceae
Sanskrit name: Nimba
Hindi name: Neem

❈

Possessed of many and great virtues, this native Indian tree has been identified on five-thousand-year-old seals excavated from the Indus Valley civilization.

India's earliest societies used margosa or neem leaves to exorcise the spirits of the dead, as described in the first century by the Akanaru manuscript:

Having put on indigo
And bitter neem leaves
They bring me to the god
Fearful in his eminence.
Bowing before him
They sing of his tree
And, shaking,
Dance all night.

Today the margosa is valued more highly for its capacity to exorcise the demons of disease than the spirits of the dead, and an image of the folk goddess Sitala can often be seen suspended from a margosa branch where she guards against smallpox, once the great killer of the Indian countryside. With the eradication of smallpox, now bathing in a margosa-leaf infusion, excellent for soothing scabs and clearing away scars, marks the ritual termination of an attack of chicken pox or measles.

Renowned for its antiseptic and disinfectant properties, the tree is thought to be particularly protective of women and children. Delivery chambers are fumigated with its

burning bark.* Dried margosa leaves are burned as a mosquito repellent. Fresh leaves, notorious for their bitterness, are cooked and eaten to gain immunity from malaria.

This tree, so beloved of India—with its fine starlike flowers, its long lime-colored berries, and its feathery crests tossing fifty feet into the sky—is an invaluable natural pesticide and its oil is used to protect the bark of other trees from termites. For centuries its leaves have been used to store grain, or to preserve papers and clothes. Ecologically sympathetic, the classical texts of Indian architecture even call the margosa "Earth's Wish-Fulfilling Tree" because its inflorescence is purifying and its termite-resistant timber is invaluable to house construction in the tropics.

More mundanely, the tree is revered by Indian herdsmen as a gentle but effective veterinary poultice, a virtue confirmed by the sixteenth-century Portuguese botanist and traveler, Garcia da Orta in his *Coloquios*:

Doctor R.:   I beg you to recall the tree by the help of which you cured that valuable horse.

Orta: It is a tree that has great repute as valuable and medicinal. . . . The sore backs of horses that were most difficult to clean and heal were very quickly cured . . . with leaves pounded and put over the sores, mixt with lemon juice.

* Margosa seed oil has been clinically tested as an external contraceptive, used by women as a spermicide.

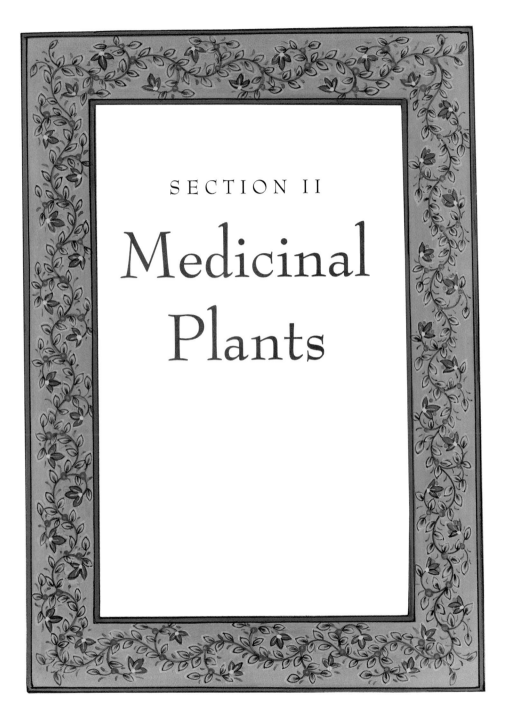

SECTION II

Medicinal Plants

MEDICINAL PLANTS

A remarkable feature of Charaka's great treatise is its theory of classification. One section classifies substances and phenomena into rational groups, which include the days of the solar calendar, seasons, topography, rainfall, vegetation, or the individual characteristics of habitable land. Another classifies all living creatures according to the manner of their birth—born of the womb, of eggs, of heat and moisture, of seeds. These are further subdivided into a long list of known creatures ranging from parasites and reptiles to herbivorous and carnivorous animals, and how elements of each may contribute to the lives of others.

But the treatise is most exacting in its classification of those living things born of seeds—the plants and trees, which are the laboratory of Ayurvedic medicine. After identifying almost 1,500 plants as belonging to four types according to their fruits and flowers, and whether they are annuals or perennials, Charaka then isolates the 350 plants useful to Ayurvedic medicine.

The medicinal plants are divided into fifty groups, according to the physiological actions of the medicines that can be extracted from them. These fifty groups cover everything from curatives to preventives, and Charaka is careful to remind readers of his treatise that plants powerful enough to cure disease are often the very plants which are most poisonous when used by those who do not understand their properties. He cautions against quacks and fake doctors. He classifies many of the poisonous actions of Ayurvedic plants. He identifies the seasons and times of day when a particular plant's medicinal powers achieve their maximum potency, indicating when it should be collected. He describes which parts of a plant can be used profitably, which should be left strictly alone. Since true Ayurvedic medicine is a compound of plant extracts mixed according to exact measurements and specifications, Charaka stresses that death by plant poisoning can be an extreme result of improper treatment.

The plants described by Charaka present a sound cross-section of India's medicinal herbs, shrubs, and trees, ranging from diuretics, cardiac tonics, and plant extracts capable of knitting together bone fractures to plants that increase fertility both in men and women, bronchodilators, purgatives, digestives, or antidotes to poisoning.

Many of these plants are still widely used in Ayurvedic prescriptions, their reputation as medicines further enhanced by contemporary clinical tests that have confirmed Ayurveda's claims for the brain tonic of the Indian pennywort, the bronchodilatory effects of the Bel, the diuretic properties of hogweed, the anticholesterol action of the Indian bedellium, and so on.

Modern science still extracts most of its medicines from plants, and yet, in this age of galloping information, people know less and less about the medicinal value of plants. Ayurveda encourages all human beings to learn about medicinal herbs and plants, ideally growing and preserving them as well, for their own well-being and the well-being of future generations.

12
Indian Pennywort

(*Centella asiatica*)
Family: Umbelliferae
Sanskrit name: Brahmi
Hindi name: Brahmi

A double blind clinical test was conducted on 30 mentally retarded children who were free from epilepsy and other neurological conditions to study the effect of the drug (extracted from Indian pennywort) *on general mental ability.*

The results indicated a significant improvement in both general ability and behavioral patterns when the drug was administered for a short period of 12 weeks.

Appa Rao (1973), *Medicinal Plants of India*, Indian Council of Medical Research (1987)

⸙

*T*railing across the ground and rooting at the nodes, this herb grows wild in India, especially in marshlands and alongside water reservoirs where it is collected by hand for the use of Ayurvedic doctors.

Patients suffering from protein deficiencies and nervous disorders are administered drugs extracted from Indian pennywort and modern clinical tests have studied the anabolic effect of these drugs, proving they do increase red blood corpuscles, vital capacity, and total protein, while the increase in the hemoglobin percentage is statistically significant.

But Charaka states the true value of the Indian pennywort lies in its outstanding performance against senile decay and loss of memory, and its capacity for enhancing verbal articulation. Among the original medicines of the Ayurveda, the herb was known and used by the great sages of Indian philosophy, who named it *brahmi*, or knowledge. According to the Taittiriya Upanishad:

For truly, here beings are born from knowledge.
Born, they live by knowledge.
When departing, into knowledge they enter.
Knowing this, the student approached the knower, saying:
Sir, teach me.

13
Asparagus Racemosus

(*Asparagus racemosus*)
Family: Liliaceae
Sanskrit name: Satavari
Hindi name: Satavar

Who put the seed in man saying, Let this
thread of life be spun?

Atharva-Veda (circa 1000 B.C.)

❧

The classical Indian names for the asparagus racemosus indicate its main interest to Ayurvedic medicine—the capacity to increase a man's fertility. In Sanskrit the plant is called the "Hundred Rooted" or the "Many Heired," and contemporary clinical tests have shown that these succulent tubers actually do increase the male sperm count, as their ancient names suggest.

A graceful and delicate climbing plant that grows wild in the lowland Indian jungle, asparagus racemosus is also grown in gardens or in terra-cotta pots on Indian porches for its tubers or roots, which are rich in vitamin A. These are eaten in salads, vegetable dishes, or as candied sweets, and regarded by Indian housewives as good for vision, particularly in curing night blindness. Nutritive as well as antidiarrheal and antidysenteric, the tubers are also thought to have aphrodisiac qualities.

The bark is poisonous, but the leaves are boiled to form part of an Ayurvedic poultice applied for the relief of boils, while the root taken with milk is considered helpful in recovering from gonorrhea.

The plant is popular with nursing mothers for its lactogenic properties, and also cultivated for grazing cattle, as the asparagus racemosus has even been found to increase a cow's milk.

14
Asoka

(Saraca asoca)
Family: Caesalpinaceae
Sanskrit name: Ashoka
Hindi name: Ashok

❧

The Indian spring is not a soft season, nor is its color green. It is the season of fertility, when the red blossoms of flowering trees open toward the red sun of summer. Its predominant color is red, the color of the fulfilled woman, worn as the auspicious mark on her forehead.

And yet the tree most intimately associated with women in India's mythology is the evergreen asoka; decoctions made from its bark are used to soothe menstrual cramps and prevent excessive blood loss during menstruation. The bark decoction also relieves the pain and tension related to menopause.

The mythological relationship between trees and women descends from the prehistorical inhabitants of India, when people propitiated the spirits which inhabited the jungle, sensing the deep connections between plants and human beings. To illustrate this mutual dependency, early tribal myths tell of women fertilizing trees. The asoka is supposed to burst into flower when kicked by a virgin's foot, the mango tree at the touch of her fingers.

This image of a young woman and a tree constantly recurs in Indian art, and trees are supposed to increase both desire and fertility in a woman. But the asoka also contributes to the health of men. Asoka bark is noted for its astringent and styptic properties and a lotion made from the bark is used to heal open wounds. Its flower buds, which are highly nutritious, are eaten in the last month of the year by men and women alike, to remove grief.

The very name asoka means "unsorrowing." It is said that when her time was near, the mother of the Buddha went deep into the forest of Lumbini. There, clinging onto an asoka tree, she gave birth to the Enlightened One.

15
Castor

(*Ricinus communis*)
Family: Euphorbiaceae
Sanskrit name: Eranda
Hindi name: Rendi

❧

*She is become
the light of her house:
a red flame in the bowl
of a shining oil lamp.
She has given birth to
his son, whose lands are
made lovely with flowers
by the pattering rain.*

Ainkurunuru
(circa third century A.D.)

*E*arly in its evolution, Indian medical science recognized the existence of both rheumatoid arthritis and sciatica. From that time Ayurvedic physicians have used the castor plant's oil and powdered root in medicinal compounds for lumbago, pleurodynia, sciatica, and rheumatism, both for external application and for internal medicine in the forms of pills and liquids. This knowledge entered the Arab pharmacopoeia, where castor was called "the sesame of India."

Castor is one of the first medicinal plants known to man. Its seeds have been found in Egyptian tombs dating to 4000 B.C. and mentioned in papyrus scrolls thought to have been written around 1500 B.C. Four centuries before the birth of Christ, the Greek historian Herodotus noted its use as a lamp oil, a purpose for which it is still employed in the temples of south India. The lampblack produced by the combination of castor oil with wicks dipped in herbal preparations has provided the universal eye cosmetic of India known as kohl, each Ayurvedic clinic making its own version of this medicated lampblack.

Europeans only became familiar with the plant around the eighteenth century, for the laxative provided by castor oil. Ayurveda records castor's value as a purgative from several millennia earlier, and recommends small doses as particularly useful for vulnerable patients such as very young children, women immediately after childbirth, and pregnant women.

Ayurveda notes the close connection between the castor plant and the nursing mother. The leaves of the castor plant are warmed and applied to a woman's breasts as a galactagogue, i.e., to increase the secretion of milk. The oil is rubbed over a nursing mother's nipples each time a child is removed from the breast to prevent soreness, and the leaf also provides Ayurvedic doctors with one of the ingredients used in a mixture which is drunk by a woman to increase milk flow.

Additionally, castor oil is an excellent hair tonic and is rubbed into the nursing mother's scalp to encourage luxuriant hair growth after the rigors of childbirth, and also as a massage oil to renew her strength and remove the aches and pains of childbirth.

16

Indian Gentian

(*Andrographis paniculata*)
Family: Acanthaceae
Sanskrit name: Kalamegha
Hindi name: Kalmegh

3 to 6 Kirata tablets or pills, each of 5 grains, are given every morning with water and honey, according to the virulence of attacks in malaria. Brigade Surgeon G. G. Hunter considers this superior to quinine.

Dr. K. M. Nadkarni,
Indian Materia Medica (1908)

❧

A classic injunction by Charaka is that Ayurvedic pharmacologists should always consult the living herbals of those in close touch with nature. The Indian gentian is a case in point. Long before it reached the pages of Charaka's treatise, and millennia before it entered the herbal drug lists of the outside world, the action of this Himalayan herb on fevers had been perceived and put to use by a tribe called the Kiratas, who lived deep in the Indian forests. Indeed, the Sanskrit synonym for Indian gentian is *Kirata Tikta* or "the bitter plant of the Kirata," and a bitter infusion made from its dried twigs is still a widely used remedy against the fevers and agues of malarial attacks.

Malaria has been a persistent scourge in India, carried by mosquitoes breeding in stagnant water. The British in India called it "swamp fever" and suffered bitterly from malarial fevers, as attested to by so many gravestones in British cemeteries all over India. The Ayurvedic medicine "chiretta," as gentian was called in English, was the only known remedy against malarial fevers until the discovery of quinine-yielding *Cinchona* trees in central South America.

Extracts from this shrub with its square stems and purple flowers are an important ingredient in a well-known Indian fever powder called "Sadurashan-Churan" sold widely in Indian bazaars. A bitter Indian gentian tonic is used to stimulate sluggish livers and to treat gout. As the plant also yields a powerful vermifuge, it is a common prescription for children suffering from worms or other stomach ailments.

17
Liquorice

(*Glycyrrhiza glabra*)
Family: Papilionaceae
Sanskrit name: Yastimadhu
Hindi name: Mulethi

If equal quantities of clarified butter, honey, sugar and liquorice be mixed with fennel-juice and milk, the nectar-like composition is said to be holy, provocative of sexual vigor, a preservative of life, and sweet to the taste.

Vatsayana, *Kama Sutra* (fifth century A.D.)

＊

Whether brought on by the freezing snowstorms of northern India's Himalayan mountains, or the sudden cold nights of Rajasthan's desert areas, Ayurvedic doctors prescribe liquorice for the ailments of the winter season.

Ayurvedic medicine recommends the root of this graceful plant with its light, feathery foliage, as beneficial in the treatment of coughs, colds, and other bronchial irritations.

Sweet-tasting dried liquorice roots are sold in every Indian bazaar, to be sucked as throat lozenges, to relieve hoarseness and coughs. Such is the fame of liquorice as the curative of sore throats that it remains popular as a lozenge for singers and declaimers in our own times, as it was in Charaka's day.

Powdered liquorice is also considered by Ayurvedic medicine as an excellent remedy for hyperacidity, and clinical tests by Dr. G. S. Keith conclude that "for relieving pain, discomfort and other symptoms caused by acid matter in the stomach, it is wonderful. It seems to remove the irritating effects of acids in a better way than alkalies."*

Liquorice was known not only to the ancient Egyptians and Chinese, but also to the ancient Greeks. Dioscorides, the Greek physician who authored *De Materia Medica*, recommended liquorice juice for hoarseness and for heartburn, while in an assessment independent of the *Kama Sutra*, Chinese medicine praises liquorice for "rejuvenating those who consume it for a long time."

* From Dr. K. M. Nadkarni, *Indian Materia Medica* (1908, reprinted 1992).

18
Vasaka

(*Adhatoda vasica*)
Family: Acanthaceae
Sanskrit name: Vasaka
Hindi name: Adusa

As a hawk
on its cord
is held in flight,
so life
bonded by energy
is held by breath.
Gorakhnath,
Goraksa Sataka
(circa A.D. 1100)

✠

Ayurveda produced the concept of "life breath," which was later used by the practitioners of yoga and *kundalini* yoga. Its earliest physicians established the close connection between oxygen inhalation and the neurological system, evolving various *pranayamas*, or breathing techniques, which could be used to improve the nervous system and increase mental faculties such as memory and alertness, so necessary to forestalling the body's decay. But in order to practice such techniques the human lungs had to be healthy, and for this Ayurvedic physicians used the plant vasaka.

In Ayurvedic pharmacology the main action of the vasaka is as a bronchodilator and an expectorant. The humidity in many parts of tropical India, as well as the severe winters of Indian mountain regions, have made respiratory illness a serious problem, and the importance of vasaka's remedial action in respiratory infections such as chronic bronchitis and tuberculosis was sufficiently recognized to find early international acceptance as a medicine, as noted by Buddhist medical manuscripts from fifth-century China.

Honored for its strength, in Sanskrit botany this modest shrub is named Lion's Muzzle and Stallion's Tooth after the shape and color of its flowers. But its antiseptic and pesticidal qualities justify the popular name of vasaka, which means "Little Dweller," or "protector of the dwelling place." Ayurvedic medicine has always used extracts from the vasaka plant for external applications against inflammations, neuralgia, and relief for the pains of rheumatoid arthritis.

More recently, Ayurvedic science has extracted drugs from vasaka which regulate excessive menstrual flow, and Ayurvedic physicians now regard vasaka as the rival of the asoka tree in its value to women.

19
Chebulic Myrobalan

(Terminalia chebula)
Family: Combretaceae
Sanskrit name: Haritaki
Hindi name: Harad

As a tonic for promoting strength and preventing the effects of age, chebulic myrobalan should be taken every morning with salt during the rainy season, with sugar in the autumn, with ginger in the first half of winter, with long pepper in the second half of winter, with honey in the spring, and with treacle in the hot months.

Ayurvedic prescription

Chebulic myrobalan, together with the emblic and belleric myrobalans, form the legendary "Three Fruits" of Ayurveda—a vitamin-rich combination used in all its basic health tonics. Because of their astringent and antiseptic properties, this combination is also used on surgical dressings.

Since Charaka's time, Indian physicians have extolled the virtues of chebulic myrobalan, calling restoratives which include it by such picturesque names as "The Unfailing," "The Restorative," "The Fearless Against Ill Health," "The Life Giving," and "The Animating." It was favored by such Graeco-Roman and Arab physicians as Avicenna, Scrapion, and Mesua. Through them the plant became much in demand in Europe. Indeed, so widely was it known by 1610 that in his play *The Alchemist* Ben Jonson has a character describing a lady's kiss as being, "So light, she melts/Like Myrobalane."

Apart from its value as a tonic, the dried fruits and seeds of myrobalan are prescribed in Ayurvedic medicine for such illnesses as dermatosis, edema, and urinary infections. Chebulic myrobalan is also considered an excellent blood purifier.

Finely powdered, it is used as a dentifrice, and for bleeding or ulcerated gums. Coarsely powdered and smoked in a pipe, it is used to relieve asthma.

20
Emblic Myrobalan

(*Emblica officinalis*)
Family: Euphorbiaceae
Sanskrit name: Amlaki
Hindi name: Amla

The chebulic myrobalan for resistance to disease, the embelic myrobalan for its tonic value.
Treatise of Charaka (first century A.D.)

❧

The Sanskrit name for this small tree, with its leathery leaves and fleshy fruit, translates as "The Sustainer" or "The Fruit where the Goddess of Prosperity Resides," and in Hindu religious mythology the tree is worshipped as the Earth Mother, its fruit considered so nourishing the tree is believed to be nursing mankind.

The fruit of the emblic myrobalan is one of the richest natural sources of vitamin C available in India, and is commonly described as containing twenty times the amount of vitamin C to be found in a glass of fresh orange juice. Ayurveda recommends taking a tonic made from the fruit throughout the winter months.

The fresh fruit's high concentrate of vitamin C has been shown by recent clinical tests on patients suffering from pulmonary tuberculosis to be more quickly assimilated than the synthetic vitamin. Because it is also cooling, an excellent liver tonic, and assists the body in excreting urinary waste, Ayurvedic physicians recommend drinking the juice during the summer months when the body's functions become sluggish with the heat.

One of the virtues of the fruit to Ayurvedic medicine is that it can be used both fresh and dried. Together with the chebulic and belleric myrobalans, the emblic myrobalan forms the classic three fruits which are used as the basis of almost every Ayurvedic tonic, and Ayurveda's claims for the tonic properties of the myrobalans have attracted much scientific attention in India.

A series of clinical tests on the emblic myrobalan have found the fruit contains elements which are antiviral, raise the total protein level in the body, activate the adrenaline response, and which protect against tremors and convulsions.

21
Bauhinia

(*Bauhinia variegata*)
Family: Caesalpiniaceae
Sanskrit name: Kanchnara
Hindi name: Kachnar

A not-to-be-forgotten February memory is the flowering of the Bauhinias. Both the white and pink variety look their best when the first buds appear. . . . Whenever anyone shows an interest in trees and wants to know more about them, Bauhinias are among the first I introduce them to: the leaves resemble the imprint of a camel's foot; the Latin name was given by two 16th-century German botanists, Jean and Gaspard Bauhin. They were identical twins. That sticks.

All over northern India the flowering of this tree, its leafless branches covered in a blaze of pink-white blossoms, marks the advent of spring, a delightful but short season followed by a hot summer, the monsoon rains, autumn, and winter. Ayurveda offers advice on how to adjust to these seasonal changes with their sharp changes of temperature and humidity and their attendant ailments and diseases.

February is a festive time in northern India. With the harvest in, village women now have time to go out into the jungle and collect the flowers and buds of the bauhinia, which they will dry and store for medicine. It is common knowledge that a bark decoction of bauhinia is a useful antiseptic wash for a variety of minor skin infections; an infusion of its flowers with sugar a gentle laxative; and a gargle made from the bark and pomegranate flowers a remedy for sore throats.

Besides providing seasonal household remedies, Ayurveda values this plant for its effectiveness against malarial fevers and as an antidote to snake poison. It also notes that a decoction of the powdered root is good for corpulent persons, useful for breaking down fatty deposits in the body.

But Ayurveda's main interest in the Bauhinia lies in the drugs which can be extracted from its bark and made into medicines which regularize menstrual dysfunction and glandular problems, especially of the throat.

22
Swallowwort

(*Calotropis gigantea*)
Family: Asclepiadaceae
Sanskrit name: Arka
Hindi name: Aak

The stern and sacrificial arka
Kalidasa (circa A.D. 400)

***

The arka, or swallowwort, is to all appearances a humble wayside plant, a gray-leaved fleshy weed encountered on any walk, so the casual observer might be surprised by the plant's reputation, and the manner in which its mythological, ritual, and medical uses overlap.

According to the Taittiriya school of scriptures, the gods were performing a ritual of sacrifice to the sun when they spilled a jar of scalding milk onto the earth, from which sprang the swallowwort. Named arka after the sun, the swallowwort is noted for its heating properties, and for the milky liquid that flows easily from its leaves.

Perhaps the plant's reputation for sternness in Hindu myth comes from an ancient tribal caution about the poison contained in its milky latex, but offering the leaves of the swallowwort in Hindu religious rituals is believed to enhance the good health of the sacrificer. The devout use them to pour ritual oblations to the sun, after which the leaves are burned.

Ordinary Indians of all faiths know the swallowwort's antirheumatic powers. They bind its leaves on their joints during the "seventh day celebrations of the swallowwort," which mark the last month of cold weather in the Indian calendar. The leaves of the swallowwort are also analgesic and anti-inflammatory when applied externally, while the dry powder derived from its burnt leaves and flowers is used by Ayurvedic doctors for the treatment of asthma and bronchitis.

23
Indian Laburnum

(*Cassia fistula*)
Family: Caesalpiniaceae
Sanskrit name: Aragvadha
Hindi name: Amaltas

＊＊＊

One of India's loveliest flowering trees, the indigenous Indian laburnum is thought to be the most beautiful of all the laburnums, its drooping clusters longer and its individual blooms larger than their counterparts in other regions of the world.

Indians associate the tree with the hot summer months when long drooping sprays of yellow flowers cover the laburnum in clouds of gold. Every region has its own name for the tree. A common name in northern India is "the monkey tree," because of the monkeys clambering over its branches in search of the sweet pulp which enclose the laburnum's seed pods, a pulp which is also used by humans to flavor their tobacco, and by Ayurvedic physicians in cleansing the body of its wastes.

A basic principle of Ayurvedic medicine is the maintenance of the body's health and immune systems. In order to achieve this, Ayurveda recommends a regular and systematic cleansing of toxins through the elimination of body wastes. Indeed, the cleansing strength of the Indian laburnum featured in ancient religious rituals as a defense against "the snake powers of the Three Worlds," Charaka interpreted as meaning the tree was efficacious as an antivenin against snake bites, as an antitoxin, and in expelling internal worms.

Ayurvedic medicine describes the fresh sweet pulp enclosing the laburnum's seed pods as an effective remedy for colic, while the matured pulp is used to make a gentle laxative, safe for children and pregnant women. Externally, the bark and leaves are ground into a paste for chronic skin infections. Distillations from the flowers, and decoctions made from the powdered root are given for heart diseases to enlarge the capillaries in the circulatory system.

In clinical tests on the Indian laburnum, its leaves, stem bark, and fruit pulp were all found to have antibacterial properties. The root showed antifungal activity, and the essential oils extracted from various parts of the tree showed antiviral properties.

24
Plantain

(*Musa paradisiaca*)
Family: Musaceae
Sanskrit name: Kadali-phala
Hindi name: Kela

As the sheath
and branching leaves
of the plantain
are seen in its stem,
so You are the stem
of the universe
and all is visible
in You.

Prayer to the
Preserver

⁂

To Indians this tree is synonymous with plenitude. It is frequently planted in back-yards so that its fruit, combs of bananas, can be offered to the gods in gratitude for the fertility with which they have blessed the earth.

In many parts of India the plantain is regarded as a reincarnation of the Goddess of Plenty herself, and whole living trees are made an integral part of the marriage ceremony (see frontispiece). Their tapering trunks and generous leaves ceremoniously flank the entrance to the marriage arena. The posts and canopy of the wedding pavilion are made from its branches and leaves. The bridegroom is depicted in paintings as the plantain's heavy crimson flowers, the bride blessed with clusters of bananas.

The plantain is also famed for its medical uses. Taken orally, fresh plantain sap is a purgative. When applied locally, it is a styptic. Because its leaves are easily disinfected, they are used as poultices for open wounds. The dense-textured flowers are eaten as a delicacy, but when raw they are powdered into a medicine for gynecological ailments. The green fruit is valued for its astringent and cooling qualities. The ripe banana, universally known to be rich in minerals and vitamins, is often pulped and given to convalescing patients because it is easily digestible, soothing the mucous membranes and providing a nutrient for hemoglobin.

25
Eclipta Alba

(*Eclipta alba*)
Family: Asteraceae
Sanskrit name: Bhringaraja
Hindi name: Bhangra

⚜

Charaka advises taking the juice of eclipta alba with honey to prevent the onset of senility, and its oil as the best medicated massage oils for rejuvenation therapies.

There are three kinds of eclipta alba—the white-flowering, the yellow-flowering, and the black-fruiting, but all three grow throughout India by marshes, rivers, and lakes or on the foothills of the Himalayas.

Contemporary clinical tests have shown this herb contains the alkaloid ecliptine, lactones or sulfur-containing peptides, and the antiviral agent glucoside. These properties may explain why Ayurveda has effectively used medicines extracted from this plant in the treatment of jaundice. Indeed, the traditional belief in India is that extracts from the leaf can cure jaundice in a week, and Indian liver tonics always contain this herb. Powder made from its roots are used against enlargement of the liver and spleen.

Externally, eclipta alba not only provides a valuable medicated massage oil, but it is used all over India as a hair oil. Its Sanskrit synonym, *Keshraja*, means "the king of hair," and Indian women, who pride themselves on the length of their hair, have traditionally massaged oil of eclipta alba into their scalps to add luster.

A combination of the root powder and oil are rubbed on the forehead for headaches, and the plant's pain-killing property is also recognized in the leaf poultice used for scorpion stings, while a vapor bath from its leaves is considered the time-tested cure for hemorrhoids.

26
Hogweed

(*Boerhaavia diffusa*)
Family: Nyctaginaceae
Sanskrit name: Punarnava
Hindi name: Gadahpurna

The white variety is efficient in oedema (water retention), anemia, heart disease, cough, and intestinal colic.

Dhanwantari Nighantu, Ayurvedic text, (circa A.D. 1150)

The drug in the form of a powder or an aqueous decoction was found to be useful in the treatment of nephrotic (kidney) syndrome in 22 patients. The drug compared well with known drugs like corticosteroids. The drug induced diuresis (increased urine flow) in these patients. Besides relief in clinical oedema, these patients also showed an overall improvement such as decrease in albumin urea, rise in serum protein, and fall in serum cholesterol level.

Clinical observations by Singh and Udupa (1972), *Medicinal Plants of India*, Indian Council of Medical Research (1987)

The hogweed flourishes annually when the heat of summer is dispersed by the season of the rains, and is commonly called by Indians "The Renewed Herb" or "The Rain Born." Unlike its unprepossessing English name of hogweed, in classical Sanskrit texts this plant is known as "The Detector of Edemas," which indicate kidney disease.

Hogweed has a long tradition in Ayurvedic medical practice. Charaka used it to make a decoction for dissolving kidney stones. The Ayurvedic surgeon Susruta mentions its use in snake-poisoning and rat-bite infections. Another great Ayurvedic physician, Chakradatta, used it to treat chronic alcoholics, while medieval physicians traditionally prescribed it for fevers in patients suffering from urethritis, as well as for asthma and jaundice.

It is now believed that Ayurvedic physicians defined a single hogweed plant with different colored flowers as three separate plants possessing similar medicinal properties. However, Ayurvedic texts do identify the medicinal specialties of each, and the white-flowered variety of hogweed is thought to be the most effective.

Today, as in the past, Ayurvedic doctors primarily prescribe drugs made from the white-flowering hogweed to dissolve kidney stones and induce urination.

27

Indian Madder

(*Rubia cordifolia*)
Family: Rubiaceae
Sanskrit name: Manjishtha
Hindi name: Manjith

In him floods turned in all directions like rivers—red and copper-dark, running all ways in a man, upward and downward.

Atharva-Veda (circa 1000 B.C.)

⁜

The very word for color in India's classical languages derives from red, and Indian madder is the true Indian red, a color which symbolizes blood and energy. It is equally the sign of the menstrual cycle of the fertile woman, who marks her forehead red to show her status, and the ruby worn on the arm band of a warrior king, the red of blood and power in battle.

Chemistry and botany are deeply linked in Ayurveda. In the evolution of the medical science some extracts of a plant were turned into colors for dyes, tanning, etcetera, while other extracts were examined for their pharmacological attributes.

The root of the Indian madder plant was discovered to be of medicinal value by Ayurvedic physicians, and as befits a plant which is synonymous with red, the medicinal properties of the Indian madder root were found to lie largely in their actions on the blood. Powdered and made into prescriptions, the Indian madder root provides a valued blood purifier, particularly prescribed to women experiencing menstrual irregularities and in an infusion for women after the delivery of a child. It is also prescribed against blood dysentery, internal inflammations—medieval European physicians gave decoctions of madder root, known as wound drinks, to patients "who had fallen from high places" and were suffering internal injuries—and for urinary disorders.

Earlier in this century, during the 1920s and 1930s, a series of European doctors conducted tests on the medicinal properties of the madder root and came to some interesting conclusions. Dr. Matthilous considered it to be effective in regulating the menstrual cycle as did Dr. Hufeland, who also prescribed it for rickets. Both these drug actions were acknowledged by Dr. A. Bauer, who also felt the calcium content of the madder root recommended it as a drug for patients suffering from tuberculosis, while its special acid—ruberythrinic acid—was so effective in turning urine sufficiently acid to dissolve stones in the urinary tract that Dr. Bauer felt any operation to eliminate such stones should invariably be delayed until a course of madder has been carried out so as to try and dissolve the calculi by ruberythrinic acid and thus remove them by the natural outlet.

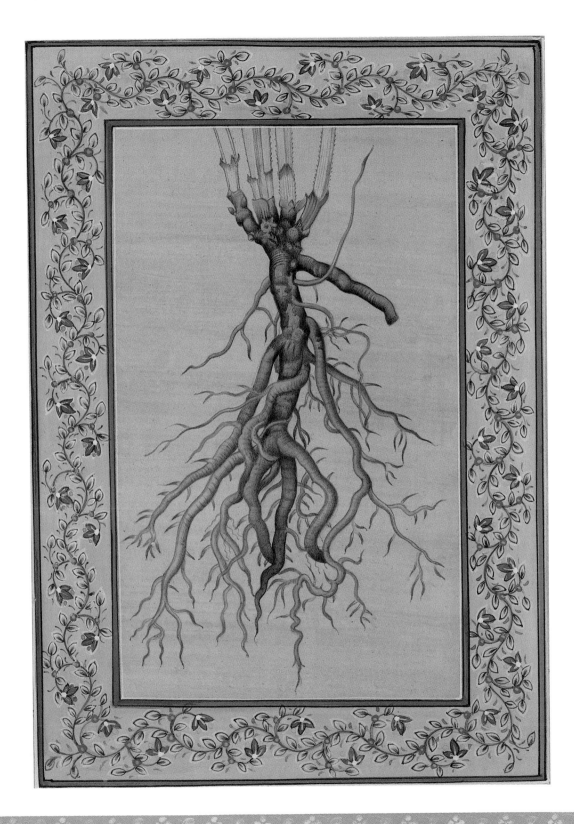

28
Arjun

(Terminalia arjuna)
Family: Combretaceae
Sanskrit name: Arjuna
Hindi name: Arjun

⁂

As early as 800 B.C. there are allusions to the arjun's function in religious offerings, and ancient Hindu scriptures describe the arjun as combining the virtues and the essences of all herbs.

A sturdy tree with silver-white bark, the arjun's great service to medicine lies in its bark extract, which is used in the clinical treatment of hypertension. A powder from the bark, taken orally, is a valuable cardiac tonic.

But in central India, the home of the arjun, the tree is less worshipped than loved for being the commoner's friend.

According to a legend, the King of Tree Spirits had two sons. One day, heated with wine, the sons stripped off their clothes and made for the river in laughing pursuit of a group of celestial maidens. They were just gaining in the chase when a sage passed by. Because they ignored him, the insulted sage cursed the young men, and they were turned into arjun trees, condemned to pay for their arrogance by having their wood used for such utilitarian purposes as boat building, tanning, and the making of agricultural implements and weaponry.

Nonetheless, the felling of an arjun tree is affectionately ritualized. The chosen tree is propitiated with offerings the night before it is cut down. Then at dawn the tree is sprinkled with holy water, the ax man's blade honed with butter and honey, the tree felled with prayers, and its timber used to carve a religious image before performing any other function.

The arjun tree's medicinal value comes from its uses in cardiac drugs, and it is mankind's good fortune that the agitations of the heart, which condemned the sons of the King of Tree Spirits to become arjun trees, also produced remedies for the ailments of the human heart.

29 ❧ Indian Bedellium

(*Commiphora mukul*)

Family: Burseraceae

Sanskrit name: Guggulu

Hindi name: Guggal

Preliminary clinical tests were carried out on 22 patients of hypercholesterolemia associated with obesity, ischaemic heart disease, hypertension, diabetes. . . . Crude guggulu (Indian bedellium) was administered orally . . . in divided doses for 15 days to one month. A fall in total serum cholesterol and serum lipid-phosphorus was noted in all the cases. . . . The body weight also revealed a significant decline in 10 patients of obesity.

Satyavati (1966), Dwarkanath and Satyavati (1970), *Medicinal Plants of India*, Indian Council of Medical Research (1987)

Further studies in 12 cases of hyperlipaemia (9 associated with obesity, 2 of ischaemic heart disease and one of cerebral thrombosis) showed that oral administration of crude guggulu (Indian bedellium) could effectively lower the serum turbidity and also prolong the coagulation time in all 12 cases.

Sastri (1967), Tripathi et al (1968), *Medicinal Plants of India*, Indian Council of Medical Research (1987)

This thorny plant, which seldom grows higher than six feet, is found in the semidesert areas of India. During the winter months incisions are made in its greenish yellow outer bark, to release a fragrant golden resin known from ancient times as an important source of Indian medicine.

Originally, the fragrant resin which burns in fire, melts in the sun, and forms a milky emulsion when stirred in hot water, was used for religious ritual. It is mentioned in the earliest instructions for performing Hindu religious oblations, and it was traditionally burned by Indian virgins in rituals designed to enamor potential bridegrooms.

There are almost eighty species of the plant, some yielding the myrrh of biblical times, and its value as an incense was known from India to Greece. The records of Periplus show the resin was being traded between India and Greece in the first century A.D., the very time when Charaka was describing its medicinal actions in his treatise.

The only part of the Indian bedellium used by Ayurvedic medicine is the fragrant oleoresin, from which are extracted drugs for the treatment of arthritis, water retention, rheumatism, and glandular and neurological disorders.

Contemporary clinical tests have located a steroid fraction in the resin, which has proved as effective in the treatment of secondary arthritis problems as hydrocortisone, as well as a highly potent anti-inflammatory agent.

Charaka also refers to the drug action of this resin in reducing obesity and its attendant perils, his observations repeatedly confirmed by Ayurvedic physicians through the centuries.

30 ❧ Thorn Apple

(*Datura alba*)
Family: Solanaceae
Sanskrit name: Dhatura
Hindi name: Dhatura

If food be mixed with the fruit of the thorn apple, it intoxicates.

Kama Sutra (fifth century A.D.)

The Indian thorn apple, or datura as it is known locally, seems the most indigenous of Indian shrubs, growing wild over the foothills of the Himalayas in rank soil and wasteland. Yet, it probably arrived in India from Greece—where its leaves were thought to have been used for prophecy by the priests of the Delphic Oracle—the seeds buried in the earth that was carried as ballast on trading ships. Another theory suggests the seeds were scattered by the traveling gypsy caravans which moved between India and the plant's native habitat on the borders of the Caspian Sea. However, when the thorn apple first made its appearance, ancient Indians were familiar with its fruit, and early Ayurvedic physicians were well aware of the toxic properties of the seeds.

The entire plant has properties similar to those of belladonna, only stronger, and medicines made from thorn apple were administered by Ayurvedic doctors with extreme caution, as an overdose could cause fatal poisoning.

Indeed, by the time the British arrived in India the poisonous seeds of the thorn apple were the drug of choice for homicidal and suicidal Indians, and the annual medical records of territories administered by the British Empire teem with cases of the criminal use of datura poisoning in murders. Even today, a common reason for death in the areas where this plant grows wild, is among children eating the half-ripe seeds.

The flowers, with their large white corollas, have narcotic and sedative properties, which make them popular intoxicants, but which are administered by Ayurvedic physicians in drugs for patients suffering from cerebral or mental disorders, as well as to allay spasmodic bronchial asthma, coughing fits in whooping cough, and spasms of the bladder.

The datura's narcotic properties are even more evident in the leaves, which are either powdered or rolled and smoked, for the alleviation of asthma, or in its toxic seeds, which are crushed and applied externally to the sexual organs for aphrodisiac purposes.

Interestingly, for the treatment of hydrophobia (rabies) Ayurvedic medicine prescribes a tincture of datura seeds taken internally. Modern laboratory tests have identified the element which produces datura's sedative effect as stramonium, and recent articles in Western medical journals have urged further studies on stramonium's effectiveness as a remedy for hydrophobia, on the grounds that no other drug deserves a more thorough and careful trial for treating this dreadful disease, spread by rabid animals, for which medicine still has no cure.

31
Winter Cherry

(*Withania somnifera*)
Family: Solanaceae
Sanskrit name: Ashvagandha
Hindi name: Asagandh

The Western name of this plant is misleading, implying with the word "cherry" that the fruit is edible, but the seeds contained in the fruit of the winter cherry are poisonous, and Ayurvedic medicine uses only the root and leaves for its drugs.

These have now been tested and found to contain three alkaloids, including the bitter somniferin, which has hypnotic properties. An infusion made from the leaves is given by Ayurvedic physicians, aware of the medicine's narcotic properties, to patients suffering from fevers or stress.

The root, on the other hand, is powdered and used as an invigorating and nutritive tonic not only for healthy infants and growing children but even to restore the health of children emaciated by famine. Ayurvedic physicians also believe the root can significantly improve the sperm count of patients suffering from seminal inadequacies, and perhaps its tonic properties have contributed to the traditional belief that the powdered root is aphrodisiac when taken with milk or clarified butter.

Charaka praises the effect of drugs compounded from the root of the winter cherry when used systemically against wasting diseases, as well their effect when applied externally as ointments and fomentations for skin diseases, especially leukoderma.

A modest shrub, the winter cherry recurs in almost all Ayurvedic prescriptions for tonics for general debility, and its properties are considered particularly useful for improving memory lapses in the elderly, or for patients who are recovering from such diseases as rheumatic fever and consumption, and for pregnant women.

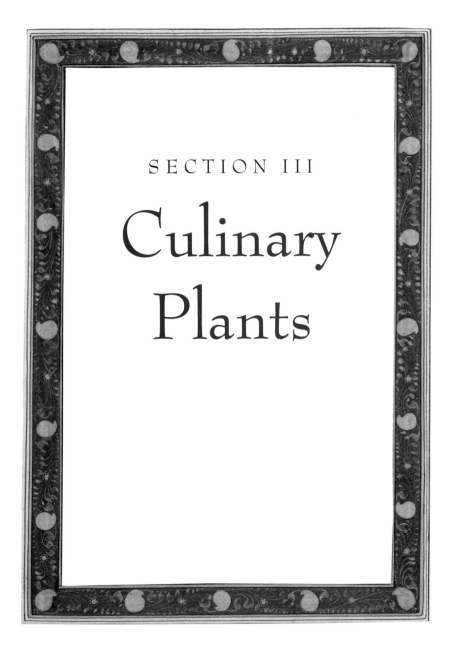

SECTION III

Culinary
Plants

CULINARY PLANTS

*D*ietetics form an integral part of Charaka's treatise and six sections are devoted to the discussion of diet and disease. In a later chapter on digestion, Charaka asserts that the life process itself depends on what a man consumes.

What appears an obvious observation is then examined through the lens of Charaka's Theory of Classification. Edible and potable substances are divided into a series of sections which identify all the various kinds of drinking water—an important classification even today, when half the diseases in all underdeveloped countries are still spread by water—continuing through various species of cereals, legumes, salts, spices, herbs, fish, meats, milk products, cooking oils, and so on, ending with a classification of alcoholic beverages.

Charaka describes the digestibility, nutritional value, and medicinal action of several hundred edible and potable substances, observing how these substances can be rendered harmful or nutritively enhanced by the way in which they are prepared or cooked, or by the manner in which they are combined with other foods, or the quantities in which they are taken, or the season and local climate where they are consumed.

By the time Charaka wrote his thesis on medicine, a large part of India's population was already vegetarian in its eating habits, influenced by the two pacifist religions, Buddhism and Jainism, which specifically banned killing an animal for food. This vegetarian population was conscious of the connection between diet and health, and their knowledge was reflected in their cooking. Even today one of the great joys of Indian food lies in its wide variety of vegetarian cuisines based on local spices, vegetables, and cooking oils.

Travelers, and the exchange of medical knowledge required by Ayurvedic practice, meant that an evolving body of information about edible and medicinal plants was conveyed not just through the Indian subcontinent but far beyond the borders of India through trade with other ancient cultures, centuries before Charaka set down Ayurveda's principles in a treatise.

The reputation of Indian spices, particularly their capacity to preserve meats and other foods, was already common knowledge in most of the civilized world by the thirteenth century, when the first waves of Islamic settlers came to India bringing their barbecued meats, which were to give India a new cuisine—Indo-Islamic cooking. This cuisine included many meat, fowl, and fish dishes. Different forms of bread were introduced to the Indian diet, their flavor enhanced by Indian spices. And the cooking of Central Asia, with its monotonous concentration on meats, was vastly enlarged by India's vegetable cuisine.

Even today the Indian housewife's kitchen pays homage to India's knowledge of vegetables and spices. Above her stove there is usually pinned a picture of the Goddess of Grain—who provides the rice and wheat which are India's two staples. A balanced diet based on seasonal vegetables is the basis of her cooking, and Ayurveda's advice on nutrients and medicines is visible in the household remedies and preserves, the spices and cooking oils, the curatives and tonics which are present on her shelves. She cannot help but be attuned to India's consciousness of the connection between mankind and his food, whether it is reflected in the tradition that derives from Charaka's treatise, or the awareness that derives from such central philosophical texts of India as the Upanishads and their description of the Creation, such as this one from the Taittiriya scriptures:

From This arose Space;
From Space, Wind;
From Wind, Fire;
From Fire, Water;
From Water, Earth;
From Earth, Plants;
From Plants, Nutriment;
From Nutriment, Man.

32
Cumin

(*Cuminum cyminum*)
Family: Umbelliferae
Sanskrit name: Jiraka
Hindi name: Jeera

Grind cuminseeds very fine. Add a drop of clarified butter and a pinch of sea salt. Grind fine again. Wet and apply . . . for scorpion stings.

Treatise of Charaka (first century A.D.)

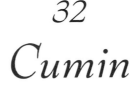

The flowers of this small, scented herb open in parasols, transmitting their aroma to the seed, a simple, unassertive spice used by Indians to season curries, pickles, or breads.

Among the earliest seasonings cultivated by mankind, the great virtue of the cuminseed lies in its digestive properties when roasted. Sometimes it is also crushed to enhance its medicinal value in counteracting dyspepsia. Because it is so easily digested and so effective in the expelling of gas from the stomach and the intestines, cumin is prescribed by Ayurvedic doctors for chronic dysentery and diarrhea, and commonly used by Indian mothers to make gripe water for their infants.

Indians consider cumin a necessary seasoning in food for convalescing patients. It is also traditional to the diets of pregnant women as an effective antidote to morning sickness. Nursing mothers find cumin lactogenic, increasing the flow of mother's milk, while its oil is effective against eczema.

In medieval times cumin had a considerable trade value as one of the fabled spices of India, the aromatic oil used for perfumes and liqueurs by neoclassical Europeans. By the seventeenth century the roasted seeds were a great favorite both in the Islamic cooking of the Ottoman Empire, and in the bread and cake recipes of European courts.

But in India, cuminseed is cooked in street snacks and banquets alike, or mixed into lemonade or tamarind water as a cooling, appetizing, and healthy protection against the discomforts of indigestion, or the hazards of waterborne stomach infections so common during tropical summers.

33 ☙ Black Pepper

(*Piper nigrum*)
Family: Piperaceae
Sanskrit name: Marica
Hindi name: Kalimrich

Once, during the height of Portuguese trade, the growers of black pepper ran in alarm to their sovereign, the Zamorin of Calicut.

"Portuguese merchantmen are not just stowing away our pepper. They are uprooting and carrying off the very pepper vines themselves!"

"Let them," said the Zamorin calmly. "Can the Portuguese take with them that last monsoon rain that gives the pepper its special flavor?"

Legend from Malabar

Pepper was one of the most important articles of Indian trade, and the finest black pepper, known as black gold, still comes from the Malabar coast of south India. The early Greeks imported pepper from India both as a spice and as a medicine. Hippocrates used it in his prescriptions, and the Romans mention it in their writings of the fifth century. It is said that when Attila the Hun sacked Europe, he demanded three thousand pounds of black pepper as part ransom for the city of Rome.

In India a single black pepper is often added to tea, as an aromatic for the throat, and as a stimulant, or a couple of peppers are sucked as throat lozenges. But black pepper's main culinary function is as a preservative. It is a frequent ingredient, usually in the form of whole peppercorns, in rice, meat, game, and pickles. Powdered, it is one of the main ingredients of the mixed spices that are the basis of curry powders.

Ayurvedic medicine considers black pepper harmless to the stomach and administers it for the alleviation of colds, coughs, catarrhs, and bronchial complaints, as well as in purges for worms. It is also used in preparations for constipation.

Black pepper has been an element in traditional Indian compounds against cholera. One of the constituents of black pepper is piperine, which is identical in composition to morphia. In Bengal a pill against cholera was compounded by Ayurvedic doctors from the following prescription with its capitalized prohibitions:

Take of black pepper, asafoetida and opium, each 20 grams; beat them well together and divide into 12 pills; of these give one dose every hour or two hours if required at the outset of the attack. ON ACCOUNT OF THE OPIUM THEY CONTAIN THEY SHOULD NOT BE CONTINUED TOO LONG.

34
Coriander

(*Coriandrum sativum*)
Family: Umbelliferae
Sanskrit name: Dhanyaka
Hindi name: Dhaniya

Take Coriander and Chebulic Myrobalan in equal parts. Roast on fire and make a decoction. To be taken for a week. Useful in vertigo.

Ayurvedic prescription

Mark that the juice of coriander blown up the nostrils restrains nosebleeds. . . . And coriander is effective in tremors of the heart when its powder is given with borage water.

The Herbarius Litnus (1484)*

Coriander is one of the most popular culinary plants of India. Its leaves are chopped and sprinkled over curried meats and vegetables. Its seeds are roasted and crushed to form the spices for almost all savory dishes. In some parts of India the leaves are cooked as a vegetable in themselves, and the aroma of dried coriander seeds is distinct in many Indian drinks.

Ayurvedic medicine uses coriander for numerous purposes. The plant is particularly effective as a diuretic, to increase the flow of urine, and as a refrigerant to break fevers. The crushed and roasted seeds mixed with warm water are used as a gargle in cases of thrush of the mouth, in a barley poultice for ulcers; or mixed with cold water as an eye lotion in cases of conjunctivitis.

Coriander leaves and seeds were employed as a digestive and as an aid to virility. Perhaps the latter explains the extensive trade in coriander as an aromatic stimulant and spice from very ancient times, since its seeds have been found in early Egyptian tombs.

As a medicine coriander was employed by Hippocrates and other Greek physicians, so that its medicinal values were already known by the time the Romans introduced coriander to Europe, explaining its presence in the very earliest European medical herbaria.

* German manuscript listing medicinal uses of 150 plants then available in the shops of apothecaries and spice merchants.

35
Mango

(*Mangifera indica*)
Family: Anacardiaceae
Sanskrit name: Amra
Hindi name: Aam

❧

Our fairest one,
Beauty of the garden,
O finest fruit
Of Hindustan.
Moghul Emperor Bābur,
Bābur-nāmeh (1525)

Boy, cut these mangoes and prepare them in
slices, because in that way they have a better
taste, and the chief thing is to soak them in
wine, like nectarines.

Garcia da Orta,
The Simples and Drugs of India (1563)

With its distinctive shape and succulent golden flesh the mango is perhaps India's best-known fruit. Fortunately for Indians, the mango tree fruits in the hot summer months that precede the monsoon rains. As mangoes are highly effective against sunstroke, throughout India a variety of summer drinks are made from pulped mangoes to lower body temperatures and assuage thirst during this season. Strained with black salt, molasses, and cumin, mango juice becomes panna. Mixed with milk the juice is turned into Mango Fool. The pulp is also used in decoctions for the treatment of diabetes and blood pressure problems.

Traditionally, ripe mangoes are kept in buckets of cold water. Not only does this ensure the fruit remains fresh, it also eliminates the turpentine resin in the stalk. Strongly scented, and with a slightly astringent taste in their sweetness, mangoes are rich in vitamin C. They are used in the Indian diet throughout the year. In summer when the body is losing salt through perspiration raw mangoes are sliced and eaten with salt, or they are pickled in oil and kept for the winter months as a useful antidote to colds.

But it is not just the fruit of the mango that is used in Ayurvedic medicine. Its twigs, being antiseptic, are used like toothbrushes, for oral hygiene. Infusions made from the bark are administered for diarrhea, and for excessive flow during menstruation. The large seed which defines the mango's shape is ground into a powder for countering vaginal discharge, while the seed kernel has long been acknowledged as a cure for dysentery.

36 ⊱ Bitter Gourd

(*Momordica charantia*)
Family: Cucurbitaceae
Sanskrit name: Karavela
Hindi name: Karela

There was once a mendicant whose wife, expecting her first child, expressed a strong desire for bitter gourd. One day as he went on his rounds the mendicant saw a luxuriant creeper growing above an anthill from which hung one perfect, pendulant bitter gourd. As he was about to pluck it he heard the voice of a serpent-god demanding his child in return. In time an exquisite daughter was born, but the mendicant forgot his promise and when she was fifteen his daughter disappeared from sight. The serpent-god had reclaimed his own.
Legend from Bundelkhand

The sequence of flavors in great cuisines are always plotted as attentively as the movements of a dance, and in India a meal begins almost meditatively with the savoring of a rice or bread. Then the palate is stimulated with a bitter flavor. For this purpose a popular dish in summertime is the bitter gourd.

While some Indians consider the bitter gourd an acquired taste, many others look forward to its appearance on the table, valuing the vegetable as an appetite tonic and a stimulant for sluggish livers. It is traditionally used by Ayurvedic doctors to treat anorexia, and to dissolve kidney stones resulting from dehydration during the Indian summer. Earlier, the vegetable was crushed with black pepper and applied around the eyes as an aid to night blindness. Although this cure is no longer used, the whole plant is still powdered and used as a highly effective herbal dusting powder for wounds and skin diseases.

Modern science has ascertained the bitter gourd is particularly high in vitamin C, but in the pharmacology of the Ayurveda the gourd is renowned not just for its antidiabetic action, but for its capacity to lower exaggerated sexual drive. It is also efficacious against intestinal worms, which probably explains why Indian mothers force bitter gourd down their children as ruthlessly as Western mothers insist on their children eating spinach.

37 ⊱ *Palmyra*

(Borassus flabellifer)
Family: Palmae
Sanskrit name: Tala
Hindi name: Tada

In his hand, a spear . . .
In his black hair . . . white leaf-needles
from the crest of the young palmyra
        Purananuru (circa first century A.D.)

The palmyra palm was a royal emblem of the original inhabitants of south India, and the ruler's crown was made from the pale spikes of its fanned leaves. Even today in the southernmost Indian state of Kerala these fine white knots gleam against the dark timber of temple arches on ceremonial occasions. Elsewhere the palm leaves are woven into sleeping mats and fans, or into capes by workers in the paddy fields against the violence of tropical storms.

Because so many of their religious texts are preserved on palmyra leaves, the palm is sacred to Hindus and Buddhists. For centuries, the tree was the guardian of scholarship, with palmyra leaves the material used for books and records until replaced by the discovery of paper.

The jellylike pulp of the palm's fruit and the young fruit kernels make pleasant eating, while the germinated nuts are cooked as a vegetable dish. But the great culinary value of the palmyra lies in the thick saccharine sap, which is tapped through incisions in the branches or fruit and exuded into strategically placed earthenware pots. The predawn tapping is reputed to taste like nectar. If this sweet sap is drunk immediately it is a nutrient and stimulant, being full of vitamins. It is prescribed by Ayurveda as a healthy laxative if drunk over a few days, and used as a diuretic in cases of gonorrhea, as well as for treating gastric catarrh and inflammatory infections.

More often the sap is fermented, frothing in the earthenware jars as the sun begins to climb and heat the liquid. Then it is either drunk as tadi, which the British call "toddy," or distilled into the more potent spirit known as arak. Twice a year the tree sap yields a molasses which is made into country sugar called "jaggery," the most common form of sweetening and the base for sugar candy throughout southern India. As large parts of this area of India are governed by matriarchal societies, it is hardly surprising to the local population that the female palmyra tree yields twelve times more molasses than its male counterpart.

38
Cardamom

(*Elettaria cardamomum*)
Family: Zingiberaceae
Sanskrit name: Ela
Hindi name: Ilaichi

The territories of . . . the Maharaja of the Isles produce all sorts of spices and aromatics . . . cloves, sandalwood, betel nut, nutmeg, cardamoms. . . .

Al Masoodi, Moorish navigator,

*P*rized by foreigners for their fragrant aroma and delicate taste, cardamom seeds were called "Grains of Paradise" by the epicures of Near Eastern lands. First imported by the ancient Greeks and Romans, centuries later Portuguese and other European traders took cardamom seeds from India to sell in Europe for the making of perfumes and liqueurs. Early Arabs enjoyed cardamom seeds in their coffee, a practice which continues and which explains why cardamoms are mentioned so often in Sir Richard Burton's translation of *The Arabian Nights*.

Today, many varieties of this plant, with its exotic green-and-purple-petaled flowers and its aromatic seedpod, flourish wild on the coastal hills of western India. But the original cardamom was first cultivated in south India for aromatic, culinary, and medicinal purposes.

The pharmacological value of the cardamom is to be found in the seed, which is of particular assistance against urine retention and stomach disorders. Used by Ayurvedic science as a corrective in medical compounds and to improve the flavor and the quality of pills, the seed is also known to be a tonic for the heart and as an excellent expectorant when doctors are treating respiratory diseases.

In India it is common practice to offer aromatic cardamoms at the end of a meal, as digestives and for freshening the breath. But they are also used in cooking, not just for flavoring savory dishes like curries, but also in Indian sweets, which often combine cardamoms with rose water and thickened milk.

39

Indian Cassia Lignea

Bastard Cinnamon

(Cinnamomum tamala)

Family: Lauraceae

Sanskrit name: Tamala Patra

Hindi name: Tejpatta

Common usage

Its relish . . . and the perfume the leaf yields when boiled in wine surpasses all others. It is strange and monstrous . . . in the price; for it hath risen from one denier to three hundred a pound.

Pliny (A.D. 70)

⚜

Known in India as *tamala patra*, the bark of this evergreen tree is easily distinguished from cinnamon bark. Coarser, darker, and possessing a slightly bitter taste that is more pungent and less sweet than true cinnamon, the stronger flavor of cassia lignea is even today preferred by German and Roman chocolate makers.

With its light and very distinctive flavor, the bark is a favorite Indian condiment. Throughout India it is used to flavor rice and sweet milk–rice puddings. On the coasts of eastern India it is used as a seasoning on fish gravies and vegetable greens, while in the desert reaches of western India it is used in the preparation of lentils, or mixed with hot water and black pepper and drunk as a tisane against dehydration.

By the time the Greeks and Romans first learned of the Indian cassia lignea, its medicinal and culinary properties were already held in high esteem by Ayurvedic physicians.

In the first century A.D. Charaka was prescribing its dried leaves and bark for fever, anemia, and body odor. Its seeds were crushed and mixed with honey or sugar, and administered to children for dysentery or coughs. Discovered to be of assistance in cardiac disorders, cassia lignea bark gained a reputation on ancient trade routes as an aid to rejuvenation, while the medicinal properties of its leaf were sufficiently respected to find mention in the Arabic *Materia Medica*, Avicenna's works, and the *English Pharmacopoeia*, and the leaves can still be bought in Italian drugstores.

40

Eggplant

(*Solanum melongena*)
Family: Solanaceae
Sanskrit name: Vrintaka
Hindi name: Baigun

❧

*N*ative to India, where its culinary and medicinal value had been recognized for centuries, the eggplant was taken by Arab traders to the Mediterranean in the fourteenth century, joining the European food vocabulary as the aubergine.

The alkaloid properties of the fruit can occasion allergies, but those properties are considerably diminished by marinating or roasting it, a knowledge reflected in the multitude of different ways in which this favorite Indian plant is cooked. To name only three popular Indian methods, the eggplant is marinated in turmeric, then deep-fried in mustard oil in eastern India; marinated in salt, sautéed, then simmered in yogurt in central India; roasted over a flame, then mashed with chopped ginger, green chilies, and fresh coriander leaves in northern India.

The fruit of this plant varies in shape from the large and spherical to the elongated and berrylike, and is either purple or white in color. In Bengali folklore this purple has been likened to the color of the summer sky at nightfall, and the white to the color of the summer sky at dawn. Among the first fruits used by Ayurvedic doctors, the eggplant was prescribed as a heart tonic, an appetite stimulant, and a mild laxative and diuretic. It was also considered to help with dullness of vision, and Charaka recommended the external application of its baked pulp as a cure for inflammations and swellings.

The white eggplant is known by Ayurvedic physicians to be particularly good for people suffering from diabetes, but whether white or purple, recent clinical tests have shown the eggplant is anticarcinogenic, anticonvulsant, and valuable in reducing cholesterol.

41
Drumstick

(Moringa oleifera)
Family: Moringaceae
Sanskrit name: Sigru
Hindi name: Sahajan

❧

*Earth spreads her summer sari
languidly beneath trees.
Yet drumsticks dangle still
And mango flowers.
Come. Come. Too soon
there will be little left of these.*
Rabindranath Tagore,
The Last Honey (1892)

*. . . the plant is called the Drum-stick-tree,
from the shape of the long slender fruit, which
is used as a vegetable, or in a curry, or made
into a native pickle. . . .*
Col. Henry Yule and A. C. Burnell, *Hobson-
Jobson Glossary of Colloquial Anglo-Indian Words
and Phrases* (1886)

*M*embers of the priestly class, who once believed that drumsticks excited the libido and confused the intellect, discouraged scholars or those trying to achieve an intellectual and austere life from eating this delicious fruit. Fortunately, such holy prohibitions were ignored, and in its natural habitat of south India the many-seeded pods of the drumstick continue to be a popular ingredient in curries, lentil dishes, and vegetable dishes. The flowers and the leaves, rich in vitamins, are also included in curries.

All parts of the drumstick are used in Ayurvedic medicine. The leaf, considered an important eye nutrient, is particularly rich in vitamin A, used as an aphrodisiac. And in this century drumsticks have been confirmed as a natural antibiotic and antifungal agent.

Pterygospermin, which clinical tests seem to confirm is antitubercular, has been isolated in the drumstick's root, although Ayurvedic medicine uses the root for liver disorders.

Medicines made from drumsticks are also gynecologically valuable—both to induce abortions, and in childbirth as an aid for difficult deliveries. Externally, applications compounded from drumsticks are used for leg spasms, while the seeds are ground and administered for unblocking nasal catarrhs.

42
Tamarind

(*Tamarindus indica*)
Family: Caesalpinaceae
Sanskrit name: Chincha
Hindi name: Imli

Although tamarind has been used in India from the most remote times against scurvy, it is also known for its effectiveness against mouth and throat infections. Indeed, the most famous tamarind tree in India stands over the tomb of the legendary Indian singer, Tansen, whose golden voice led the Great Moghul, the Emperor Akbar, to name Tansen one of the nine gems of his court. Four centuries later, India's finest classical singers still travel to Tansen's tomb to pluck leaves from this tamarind tree to make into throat gargles, in the hope that their voices will become as pure as their legendary predecessor's.

The pulp of the tamarind fruit, an important source of vitamin C, is a popular ingredient in the curries and preserves of south India, a region known for its punishingly hot summers. Valued as an antidote to heat stroke, tamarind pods are often preserved in salt and sold by weight so that they can be mixed with molasses and water to provide a sherbet which is both cheap and capable of lowering body temperatures. Mixed with salted water the pulp makes a laxative so gentle it is even administered to children suffering from stomach disorders.

But the tree is of greatest use to the poor tribes who inhabit the forests of India. In times of famine they husk the tamarind seeds, which are then boiled and powdered into flour to make bread. Both the leaves and the flowers of this tree are edible, and the tamarind tree is much revered by its dependents.

In the *Tribal Myths of Orissa*, retold by Verrier Elwin in 1954, it is said:

When God planted the tamarind tree and tended it, it grew long finger-like fruit. He tasted it and found it good. He decided to share it with men. When vegetables run short, He thought, they could eat it as chutney. But I shan't tell the birds about it, He decided, otherwise there won't be enough for men.

God called Man and said to him: Guard this tree well. Plant it on your hills. It will be greatly to your profit.

43
Garlic

(*Allium sativum*)
Family: Aliaceae
Sanskrit name: Rasona
Hindi name: Lasan

A certain manuscript inscribed on birch bark was found among the treasures of the Buddhist stupa at Kashgar, China . . . written by wandering Hindus in a calligraphic script that dates back to 450 A.D. Three of the seven texts it contains are medical. And of these, the first opens in praise of Garlic.

The Bower Manuscript (circa fifth century A.D.),

As a food, garlic is included in almost all forms of Indian curries, except in those eaten by very puritanical sects who fear its reputation as an aphrodisiac, or by strict vegetarians who believe that in uprooting a garlic bulb from the ground they may accidentally kill an insect.

Contemporary clinical tests have confirmed that garlic destroys bacteria. In 1944, the chemist Chester Cavallito identified the strong smell of garlic as the compound allicin, an antibiotic which has such a broad spectrum as an effective agent against disease-spreading microbes that its medicinal value is still being analyzed. Allicin is destroyed by cooking, and garlic then loses its antibiotic power, so Indians also eat garlic raw with oil and chilies as a chutney, or with salt as a blood cleanser and for nervous disorders such as headaches and hysteria.

From its very inception, Ayurveda has used garlic to treat a wide range of diseases—rheumatism; for the lung as an expectorant and powerful decongestant; for the heart to lower blood pressure and reduce high cholesterol; for the stomach, as an anthelminthic that expels round worms from the system; for gynecological problems, to regulate or bring on menstruation; and for improving the libido. Ayurveda also prescribes garlic for anorexia and for diseases of the vocal cords. Externally, garlic is applied for deafness and pain; crushed garlic fried in mustard or coconut oil is used as an antiseptic liniment, especially in the relief of scabies sores and ulcerating wounds.

Tested in the modern laboratory, garlic has been found to be antiprotozoan, antiparasitic, and antiviral, as well as antibiotic and antifungal in cases of tuberculosis and meningitis. But perhaps the most important use of this humble bulb, which Ayurveda calls "the wonder food," will be discovered when its properties in boosting the natural immune systems of the human body are fully understood.

44

Ginger

(*Zingiber officinale*)
Family: Zingiberaceae
Sanskrit name: Shunthi
Hindi name: Adrak

The universal remedy
Ayurveda

A city with the Sanskrit name for ginger is mentioned in the *Ramayana*, indicating that in 200 B.C. this city was already the capital of the ginger trade. Ginger was widely used by ancient Indian and Chinese physicians, and Confucius was known to have eaten fresh ginger with every meal as a digestive and carminative. Two and a half millennia later, records from the reign of the Great Moghul show that the Emperor Akbar did the same.

Ginger is a frequent ingredient in Indian cooking, sliced and used in preserves and chutneys, or included as an aromatic and medicinal seasoning for many vegetable and meat dishes. The Venetian traveler Marco Polo records that the finest ginger could be found on the Malabar coast of south India, and for nearly a thousand years, from 200 B.C. to A.D. 700, Arab traders monopolized western trade in ginger, conveying it in sealed earthenware jars by caravan through Asia Minor, or on ships sailing through the Arabian Sea to Egypt, leading the ancient Romans and Greeks to identify ginger as an Arabian plant.

The Ayurveda calls dried ginger the "Great Medicament" against colds, coughs, rhinitis, bronchitis, and indigestion. It is prescribed for abdominal distention, colic diarrhea, and nausea. Infused in hot water it causes sweating and is used for breaking fevers. Applied externally it relieves rheumatic pain. Crushed ginger is rubbed on the forehead for the relief of headaches, while ginger juice is India's mustard plaster, applied on children's chests when they are suffering from colds and bronchitis. Fresh ginger is chewed for sore throats and lost voices, and ginger candies are used as throat lozenges.

Contemporary medicine considers ginger a potent antidote to motion sickness, as well as being anticholesterol and an anticoagulant. However, Ayurvedic medicine notes that people suffering from hyperacidity and gastric ulcers should avoid ginger.

Besides being a digestive and of particular value against respiratory infection, ginger is also a stimulant, perhaps explaining why it was favored in the past by men such as Confucius and the Great Moghul.

45
Cinnamon

(*Cinnamomum zeylanicum*)
Family: Lauraceae
Sanskrit name: Tvak
Hindi name: Dalchini

Spikenard and saffron, calamus and
cinnamon . . .
Awake, o north wind, and come thou south;
come blow upon my garden,
that the spices thereof may flow out.
Song of Solomon, the Old Testament

*A*yurveda uses a combination of three aromatics—Indian cassia lignea, cardamom, and cinnamon—to disguise the taste of medicines. But these three aromatics occur as much in Indian cuisine as they do in Indian medicine, and mixed with hot water and honey provide the basis of the hot drink so popular with British colonials, who added rum and lemon rind to create their beloved Anglo-Indian "punch."

On its own, cinnamon, the dried inner bark of the tree, is used to add fragrance to such simple village fare as a dish of rice and lentils, and to the elaborate dishes of aristocratic cuisine. It appears in the sweets offered in ritual ceremonies to the gods. Ground cinnamon is used in coastal India to flavor fish, especially when cooking freshwater carp, while in northern India it is often used to lend aroma and color in the making of cottage cheese.

Although all parts of the cinnamon tree are aromatic, Ayurvedic medicines are made only from the cinnamon bark. The oil pressed from this bark is very similar to clove oil, providing an effective liniment which is used for headaches, rheumatic pains, early morning stiffness, and the body aches which result from winter cold or the rainy season. Like clove oil it is useful for toothaches and painful gums.

The cinnamon bark, so often found in Indian food and used in the three aromatics that flavor medicinal drafts, is also administered by Ayurvedic doctors for anorexia, bladder disorders, and as a tonic for the heart. Its most common use is as an expectorant and decongestant, and throughout eastern India, where the monsoon rains are particularly heavy and often lead to influenzalike infections, cinnamon bark is boiled in water and inhaled as a vapor for coughs, colds, and sore throats.

46
Mahua

(*Madhuca longifolia*)
Family: Sapotaceae
Sanskrit name: Madhuka
Hindi name: Mahuva

The parrots and peacocks are calling.
Jewel among knights,
Turn your horse just once.
The mahua flowers drip mahua juice.
My jewel of a knight
Turn your horse just once.

"Song of Separation,"
folk song from Rajasthan

This self-sowing tree was almost certainly among the original plants identified by the sages who gathered material for the Ayurveda. Considered one of the most important trees of the Indian forest, the mahua has been known since the remotest times for the excellent edible oil contained in its seeds. Because the oil is thick and yellowish in color, and has the important asset of solidifying almost immediately upon being expressed from the seed, the mahua is often called the "Butter Tree."

The mahua is the most important source of food for the forest dwellers who live in the hilly, rocky areas of central India and the people who roam the desert areas of western India, so although the timber is a fine building material it is hardly ever cut. The mahua tree must be guarded from animals, since deer and bears will come for miles to eat the fallen flowers oozing their sweet juice, while peacocks and parrots can often be seen pecking around the trees at sunset and dawn. Indeed, this fact is noted by hunters from the British colonial period as shown in the nineteenth-century diaries of General R. H. Keatinge: "It is common practise to sit perched on one of the trees in order to shoot the large deer which come to feed on the fallen mhowa."

The musk-scented flowers, which rise in whorls from the tips of the branches in lovely shades of rust and crimson framed by dark green leaves, can be dried and stored almost indefinitely. Prepared in the traditional manner mahua blossoms taste rather like pressed figs. Sometimes they are mixed with leaves of other plants and cooked into a vegetable dish, or made into puddings and sweetmeats. The fruit of the mahua are fleshy green berries, which contain from one to four shiny brown seeds. The outer coat is eaten as a vegetable, and the inner skin dried and ground into meal. The oil from the seeds is

used for cooking, or sold for the making of soap and candles. It is thought that systematic cultivation of these trees in the deforested regions of India, and indeed elsewhere in the world, would provide a most potent protection against famine.

Ayurvedic medicine uses mahua preparations for removing intestinal worms, in respiratory infections, and in cases of debility and emaciation. The astringent bark extract is used for dental-related problems, rheumatism, and diabetes, while the seed oil is efficacious in treating skin ailments.

The distilled juice of the flowers is considered a tonic, both nutritional and cooling, but the forest dwellers generally drink the juice in a fermented form as a wholesome spirit, which was shunned by Europeans traveling through the forest areas because "the chief objection . . . is its peculiar penetrating smell of mice."

Those Europeans who persevered and managed to acquire a taste for mahua liquor echoed the judgment made by Forsyth in his book *Highlands of Central India* (1814): "The spirit when well made, and mellowed by age, is by no means of despicable quality, resembling in some degree Irish whisky."

In 1970, Aubrey Menen's book *The Space Within the Heart* describes the celebrations of a group of forest tribals: "They were a cheerful lot, much given to dancing and getting drunk on a liquor they made themselves . . . which tasted exactly like a weak martini."

SECTION IV

Cosmetic Plants

COSMETIC PLANTS

The same cosmetics that are described in the classical Indian poetry and literature written hundreds of years ago, are still popular in India today, and many of these skin, hair, and body treatments were first identified and popularized by early practitioners of Ayurveda.

Ayurveda stresses that beauty can only emerge through health, and through the periodic cleansing of the body necessary for an individual's physical rejuvenation. As a result of this principle, all the plants from which Ayurveda extracts its cosmetics perform a medicinal and purifying function as well. For instance, the henna paste used by Indian women to color their hair and to paint the intricate patterns on their skin, which make them more desirable according to the Indian school of erotics, is the same cooling paste recommended by Ayurveda as a cure for the skin rashes brought on by summer heat.

Ayurveda lays strong emphasis on rejuvenation through the preservation of the body's natural oils, so Indian women wash their faces with a soap substitute made from turmeric that helps the skin to retain these vital oils. Also, turmeric possesses antibacterial properties that disinfect the skin while cleansing it. Other plants used in hair oils and shampoos are known to have antifungal properties, still others are known to be useful against clogged pores or scalp infections.

Ayurveda has evolved an array of oils extracted from plants for the treatment of a wide variety of illnesses. These oils are also used in Ayurveda's detoxifying treatments as skin defoliants; to raise a patient's temperature so he will excrete toxins through perspiration; to lower the patient's temperature to close the pores against external contaminants, and so on. Many of these medicinal oils have entered into traditional Indian cosmetics as massage oils. Some remove stress and fatigue while softening the skin. Other oils relieve arthritic or rheumatic pains while helping the body shed dead skin. Still others cleanse and disinfect the skin while acting as aids to the digestive system.

The traditional facial treatments used by Indian women are linked to Ayurveda's plant pharmacopoeia. There are facial treatments which heal sores, acnes, and other blemishes while beautifying the complexion. Certain cosmetics cure pigment deficiencies, others fade scars and spots.

Ayurveda has identified breath fresheners and lip colorings that also act as appetite stimulants for those suffering from anorexia and other nervous disorders linked to the stomach. There are dyes that color the hair while cleansing the scalp of its sebaceous secretions, and bath oils that soothe or stimulate, even as they improve skin tone.

Except for rare exceptions such as treatments made from the precious saffron plant, most of these plant cosmetics and beauty treatments are available to any Indian, not just the privileged. As they are natural products, the chances of unpleasant side effects are much reduced, especially when compared to those of their chemical counterparts marketed so aggressively all over the world.

In the elaborate carvings on Indian temples, from which Indian court painters once took the models for their art and which still serve to remind the modern Indian woman of the Sola Shringar, or the sixteen classical methods of adornment, many sculptures show rows of sensual women in unself-consciously romantic or erotic poses, beautifying themselves. The sculptures usually include plant motifs—a leaf, a tree, a flower, a garland—as if to remind the viewer that nature is the greatest beautician.

47
Henna

(*Lawsonia inermis*)
Family: Lythraceae
Sanskrit name: Madayantika
Hindi name: Mehndi

Thy henna lies soaking in a fine red bowl.
The love juice of henna is a lovely tint.

O Lady, who has painted thy hands?
The love juice of henna is a lovely tint.

O Lady, put thy hand on my heart.
The love juice of henna is a lovely tint.

Folk song of Rajasthan

⁂

*I*n many parts of India the night before a wedding is known as the Night of Henna, when the bride's palms and soles of her feet are decorated in elaborate floral and fertility designs with a paste made from the powdered leaves of the henna plant. The paste is also used in some regions to stain a bridegroom's palms, because the deep red color left on the skin when the dried paste is washed off is the color that symbolizes the deep love between a husband and wife.

Henna has been a popular cosmetic not just in India but in all the countries of the Near East, where it grows as a common shrub. Egyptian mummies have been found with hennaed nails. Pliny referred to the plant as the "Cypress of Egypt." Called "camphire" by the Hebrews, henna occurs in *The Song of Solomon* in the line "My beloved is unto me as a cluster of camphire in the vineyards of Engedi."

As a cosmetic, henna has a history that dates back thousands of years in India, used by women to color their hands and nails, used by men on their beards and moustaches, used by both men and women to dye and condition their hair. The flamboyant color is so loved by Indians they even dye the manes and tails of their horses with henna.

The clusters of small rosy white or red flowers which cover a henna bush are, as Solomon's song suggests, very fragrant and used to make perfumes, while sleeping on a pillow stuffed with henna flowers is considered to have a soporific effect on patients suffering from sleeplessness.

Medically, henna is considered an anti-irritant, a deodorant, and an antiseptic. It is used by Ayurvedic physicians for skin irritations such as heat rashes and skin allergies and to cool the body during the intense heat of summer. Because of this cooling property, henna leaves and flowers are made into lotions and ointments to be used externally for boils, burns, bruises, and skin inflammations, including sores from leprosy.

48
Sesame

(*Sesamum indicum*)
Family: Pedaliaceae
Sanskrit name: Tila
Hindi name: Til

❈

Until recently, that is to say until the marketing of commercial cooking oils became widespread, each Indian village had a local "oilman" to crush cooking oil from seeds. The oil could be mustard seed or castor or sesame seed or whatever the housewife's personal preference as a cooking medium. This "cold processing" technique was better for the health than buying packaged cooking oil, as it invariably included some roughage. Also the oil seed refuse provided good cattle feed.

P. D. Karunakaran, *Monograph on Cooking Mediums of India* (1991)

A sesame seed is often offered in Hindu religious ritual because it is supposed to assist in removing every particle of sin. This ritual significance has led to the traditional usage of sesame seed as a way of saying "the smallest particle that is still perceptible."

The oil expressed from this tiny seed is a vital massage oil in India where daily massages, often administered by professional masseurs, are a common part of everyday life. Apart from the rejuvenating effect of a good massage, the popularity of sesame oil as a massage oil is due to its particular effectiveness in reducing stress and fatigue. The oil is also used to make soaps, while the seeds have a sufficient perfume to be used placed between layers of perfumed dried flowers to form fragrant potpourris or to scent clothes.

Although there are several kinds of sesame seeds, the black sesame seed yields the best oil—a clear and limpid liquid that varies in color from pale yellow to dark amber, and which has no smell. Sesame seed is not liable to become rancid if properly stored, which may explain one reason for its popularity as a cooking medium in India. In many of its properties it closely resembles olive oil and is similarly utilized. Like olive oil, it is now considered an oil that lowers high cholesterol.

While praising sesame seed oil as a massage oil and a cooking medium, Ayurveda values the sesame seed for possessing medicinal properties which can be used for dysmenorrhea, especially in cases of irregular menstruation in pubescent girls. The seeds are also diuretic and therefore prescribed for urinary disorders.

49 ❧ Indian Sarsaparilla

(*Hemidesmus indicus*)
Family: Asclepiadaceae
Sanskrit name: Sariva
Hindi name: Anantmul

Plant number 274 in Charaka's classification of medicinal plants is the Indian sarsaparilla.

As a cosmetic, Charaka recommends drinking a decoction of leaves to restore color to a sallow complexion. Ayurvedic physicians are careful to identify the difference between an *infusion*, which means mixing the powder in water, and a *decoction*, which means boiling it in water, since boiling destroys the medicinal properties contained in the root bark of the sarsaparilla, from which medicines are extracted.

The root of this slender creeper provides a traditional breath freshener. On the Malabar coast of south India where Indian sarsaparilla grows wild, the root is thrown into the brass or earthenware containers which hold a household's drinking water, to sweeten the water so that its scent will freshen the mouth when the water is drunk. It is also mixed with molasses in a sherbet, and like its American counterpart, taken as a cooling drink. Indians take such sherbets for dyspepsia and loss of appetite.

The root is also used to enrich home shampoos in India's hotter regions. Most Indian women pride themselves on the length and thickness of their hair and the addition of sarsaparilla is thought to prevent prickly heat by cooling the scalp and lessening the perspiration occasioned by humidity or summer heat.

Medically, Charaka's treatise prescribes sarsaparilla for respiratory and digestive illnesses, making no mention of the plant as a cure for venereal diseases. But records show the tapering sarsaparilla root, with its brownish corklike bark, has long been used to make an infusion administered to patients suffering from all forms of syphilis, from the ulceration caused by syphilis as well as from gonorrheal neuralgia. So far clinical tests have identified the active principles of the root as an enzyme, an essential oil, and a saponin, which possess antiviral properties but none of which is thought to have any action against syphilis, although tests are still continuing to ascertain whether Indian sarsaparilla has medicinal uses valuable to curing venereal diseases.

50 ❧ *Hibiscus*

(*Hibiscus rosa-sinensis*)
Family: Malvaceae
Sanskrit name: Japakusuma
Hindi name: Gurhal

The flower is fuller in color than that of a pomegranate, and may be the size of the red rose, but the red rose . . . opens simply, whereas when this opens a stem on which other petals grow is seen like a heart among its expanded petals. . . . This is not a common matter.

Bābur, first Moghul emperor,
Bābur-nameh (1525)

The scarlet hibiscus flower is less a cosmetic for the Indian woman than an ornament, worn in the hair or behind an ear. But Chinese and Indian women have traditionally boiled the flowers and leaves of the hibiscus, then mixed the infusion with herbal oil before applying it to their hair as a stimulant to the growth of luxurious tresses. While the Chinese use the hibiscus flower's juice as an ingredient in black dye for the hair and eyebrows, Indians include hibiscus flower juice in a famous herbal oil and conditioner which is now bottled and sold throughout eastern India under the brand name Jaba Kusam. One reason for the widespread popularity of this oil is its effectiveness against dandruff.

In Hindu mythology the hibiscus is the flower offered in the worship of the Goddess and Ayurvedic medicine seems to lend credence to the particularly female virtues of this plant by prescribing it as an emmenagogue effective in promoting a woman's period. The root yields a drug which Ayurveda believes to be useful in treating venereal disease. An extract from the hibiscus flower is also used in preventing unwanted pregnancies, inhibiting the flow of semen in men, and bringing on temporary sterility in women. Ayurvedic physicians believe the anticonception properties of the drug to be effective postcoitally.

This last claim has, of course, drawn great clinical attention in India where population control is of paramount importance. In tests on male animals the period of sterility is too limited to occasion much interest as a male contraceptive, but the findings as regards a possible natural postcoital contraceptive for women have been more impressive. In one study conducted in 1974, the scientist who conducted the experiment, Tiwari, states: "An uncontrolled clinical trial using ethanolic extract of (hibiscus) flowers was carried out in 21 women in the reproductive age group by administering . . . 3 divided doses from the 7th to the 22nd day of menstrual cycle (a total of 229 cycles). Fourteen women did not have a pregnancy for 4 years whereas 7 women dropped out of the trial for various personal reasons" (*Medicinal Plants of India*, Indian Council of Medical Research, 1987).

51
Areca Nut Palm

(*Areca catechu*)
Family: Palmae
Sanskrit name: Puga
Hindi name: Supari

Even now I remember
Wine on the lip
She innocently licked . . .
And her mouth spiced still
With camphor and areca.

Bilhana,
Vicramankdev Charit
(twelfth century A.D.)

The areca, an elegant palm tree with sweet scented flowers crowned by a tuft of leaves, bears an orange-colored fruit about the size of an egg. The fruit contains the seeds, or areca nuts, known locally as supari, which are chewed as a mild intoxicant by Indians all over the subcontinent.

It is also a favorite Indian breath freshener and taken after meals by Indian nobility. The sixteenth-century Portuguese traveler and botanist, Garcia da Orta, even suggests the name of this breath freshener came from the aristocratic classes: "In Malabar . . . the Nairs [who are the gentlemen] call it areca." Over the centuries a whole craft evolved around areca nutcrackers. Parakeets, lunging tigers, racing deer, all manner of animals and personalities are represented on these nutcrackers. A man wishing to seduce a woman broke a nut for her with nutcrackers in the shape of a couple having intercourse. A warrior's nutcracker was in the shape of his steed or an attacking soldier.

But the habit of chewing areca nut crosses all class divisions. In fact, it has been calculated that the weight of areca nuts consumed every year in India is over 100,000 tons.

The dried areca nut is powdered and used as a dentifrice, forming the basis of many tooth powders in India and China. Ayurveda recommends burning the areca nut to charcoal and mixing this with a quarter part of powdered cinnamon to produce an excellent tooth powder. It also suggests a decoction made from the areca root as a cure for sore lips.

The main medical use of the areca nut is as an anthelminthic, for expelling intestinal worms. Areca has performed this function in both India and China since ancient times.

It is also thought to be effective against malaria. A Chinese name for the nut means "antimalarial panacea."

52
Soap Nut

(*Sapindus trifoliatus*)
Family: Sapindaceae
Sanskrit name: Aristaka
Hindi name: Ritha

One fruit in forty parts of water provides a hair wash which promotes the growth of hair and removes dandruff.

Assessment of a cosmetic company on this traditional shampoo

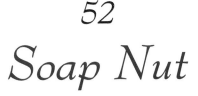

The spring of northern India is celebrated with Holi, or the Festival of Color. Participants smear orange, purple, red, green, yellow dyes, powders, and paints over each other's heads and bodies. As any visitor to India who has been a part of this festival will know, it is very difficult to rid the hair of this rainbow of colors. My own experience supports the claims made for the traditional soap-nut hair wash. Western shampoos not only do not rid the hair of these colors, they also leave the hair dry and brittle for weeks, whereas a soap-nut shampoo rinses out the colors while conditioning the hair and the scalp at the same time.

The soap nut is a large deciduous tree with fleshy fruit like a berry which yields a soap. Unlike the soaps produced by pharmaceutical companies, the substance taken from this fruit does not have a high acid content. Using the soap nut as a base, Indian women often concoct their own shampoos, frequently mixing it with a medicinal combination of the three myrobalans or other ingredients such as turmeric or coconut pulp.

It is the delicate action of the soap-nut fruit, known to Indians as ritha, which has made it the favored Indian washing medium for the most valuable fabrics and shawls. It does not bleach out the delicate natural dyes of Kashmir embroidery or harm the gold and silver threads woven into India's most expensive brocades and silks.

The seeds of the soap-nut tree yield a thick viscous oil which can cause acute nausea and acrid poisoning. This oil is used with extreme caution by Ayurvedic physicians in drugs made for patients suffering from severe cases of chronic diarrhea or cholera. Ayurveda also uses pessaries made from the fruit to induce childbirth, both for purposes of abortion and for cases of difficult delivery, while other concoctions are made into nose drops and administered through the nostrils to relieve attacks of hysteria, epilepsy, and hemicrania.

53
Turmeric

(Curcuma longa)
Family: Zingiberaceae
Sanskrit name: Haridra
Hindi name: Haldi

Take ground root of turmeric, lentil flour, a touch of pure camphor, paste of white sandalwood, and a little dried orange root. Blend. Apply on the face and body. Allow to dry. Rinse off with water.

Recipe for Uptan, a traditional skin food and cleanser

*I*ndian cosmetics pay a great deal of attention to preserving the skin's suppleness and youthful quality by retaining the body's natural oils, and where necessary augmenting them. Traditionally, an Indian, male or female, has an oil massage before bathing. Then, instead of using soap, Indians cleanse their faces and bodies of the film of oil with a moist paste made from turmeric and lentil flour. The root of the turmeric plant is known to be antiseptic and aromatic, both attractive qualities in a cleanser, but the paste also succeeds in cleansing and disinfecting the skin without drying out its natural oils. Turmeric tubers are bright yellow inside and when ground into a paste and used as a cleanser the skin takes on a golden glow, while curing skin ulcers at the same time.

The bactricidal and antiallergenic qualities of turmeric have been proved by clinical testing to have a greater medicinal effect than the merely cosmetic, which may explain its presence not just in Indian cosmetics and cleansers, but also as an essential ingredient in most Indian curries. Turmeric powder has been found to significantly increase the mucous content in gastric juices and Indian cuisine lays great weight on turmeric's therapeutic effect against gastric disorders. Used externally on animals, the volatile oil from the turmeric tuber has been found to have an anti-inflammatory effect greater than that of hydrocortisone, while other turmeric extracts have significantly reduced histamine or allergic contents in the skin, and inhibited subacute arthritis.

Taken internally as a draft, turmeric is an important ingredient in an Ayurvedic prescription for respiratory infections, which is being clinically tested at the moment to see if it can be marketed as a pharmaceutical drug.

54
Indian Kamila

(*Mallotus philippensis*)
Family: Euphorbiaceae
Sanskrit name: Kampillaka
Hindi name: Kampillaka

❦

He raised her chin
To mark her brow
With crimson,
But his trembling hand
Smudged love's sign.
She wears it thus
With pride.

Bihari (1595–1664),
court poet to Maharajah
Jai Singh of Amber,
The Satasai

This brilliant powder, a beautiful purple-red or vermilion dust made from the glands and hairs taken off the fruit of the Indian kamila (or kamala), is the most visible cosmetic of the married Hindu woman. Originally used to mark the parting of a woman's hair, then later to form a spot in the center of her forehead, the powder is placed on his wife by her husband every morning as an act of honor.

The ritual of daily honor to a wife arose from the ancient Indian view of a wife's divinity. One of the thousand symbols of the Goddess identified in a medieval Indian hymn is "the crimson sign of marriage on a woman's brow."

Traditionally a married Indian woman did not take her husband's name but the honorific *Devi*, or "Goddess." The reason for this assumption of divinity, and indeed the color of the powder marking a woman's brow—the color of blood, symbolic of fertility—is that a woman able to bear children becomes godlike. She creates and sustains life.

Oddly enough, the powder yielded by the fruit of this small evergreen tree has no medicinal properties to associate it with a woman's body. Instead, Ayurvedic science uses it to make a mixture which is violently cathartic. Causing considerable nausea and increasing the peristaltic movements of the intestines, the drug extracted from the Indian kamila is administered to rid the body of tapeworms.

55
Lime

(*Citrus medica*)
Family: Rutaceae
Sanskrit name: Nimbuka
Hindi name: Nimbu

[A lime is] about the size of a hen's egg and of the same shape . . . if a poisoned person drink the water in which its fibers have been boiled, danger is averted.

Bābur,* first Moghul emperor of India,
Bābur-nameh (1525)

⊰⊱

The most important cosmetic property possessed by the fruit of this straggling tree indigenous to India, is the concentration of vitamin C in its juice, a vitamin vital to the maintenance of healthy skin and hair. Every part of this fruit is used both in Indian cosmetics and by Ayurvedic physicians, and it is an essential part of Indian cuisine.

The lime is a traditional hair conditioner among Indians, especially during the summer when heat and humidity cause the scalp to secrete extra perspiration and oils. Then half a lime is rubbed over the scalp as a disinfectant and an astringent against sebaceous secretions. All through the year lime juice is used to remove excess grease from the hair after it has been massaged with oils, before the hair is washed with soapnut extract or other herbal preparations.

Its astringent and cooling properties also make lime juice mixed with rose water a popular skin tonic. For people with oily skins this tonic is the safest and best means of removing the greasy buildups which can cause the skin to break out in spots or other blemishes. Lime blossoms and leaves contain a fragrant oil which is used in the making of perfumes and bath oils.

As noted by the Emperor Bābur, Indian medicine uses lime juice as an antidote to the effects of poisoning. Ayurveda considers lime juice boiled with water as particularly useful against vomiting attacks and dehydration. It is also widely used to help cure coughs, and in patients suffering from anorexia, as its vitamin content makes it both a tonic and an appetizer.

* Bābur's son, the Emperor Humāyūn, notes in the book's margin that he once restored people suffering from poison with fresh lime juice.

56
Saffron

(*Crocus sativus*)
Family: Iridaceae
Sanskrit name: Kumkuma
Hindi name: Kesar

Her saffron paste
blends so perfectly
into her gold
one only knows it's there
by its fragrance.
Bihari (1595–1664),
The Satasai

Saffron is the name given to the dried stamens of the crocus plant, a plant that originated in Central Asia, but as its culinary and aesthetic virtues were extolled by Arab traders, it was soon cultivated in Persia, Arabia, Greece, the Roman Empire, India, Burma, even China.

Because so many crocus flowers are required to yield enough stamens to make even a small quantity of saffron, it was largely used by the wealthy. In Asian countries, where the yellow color produced by soaking these crocus stamens in liquid was called "the very perfection of beauty," saffron became the most valuable cosmetic, food ingredient, and dye that could be obtained.

The use of saffron as a face mask to remove pimples and soothe rashes was limited to royal women or women from the houses of wealthy aristocrats or merchants. But these ladies used it for a variety of purposes. Saffron is antiallergenic. Applied to the temples, it is a remedy for headaches. A paste made from saffron on the face and the exposed parts of the body was applied much as foundation makeup is used by women today. Not only did this saffron paste impart a smoothness to a woman's skin, it also gave the skin a golden tint, which was thought to be so desirable that pregnant women even drank saffron infused in milk in the hopes that their unborn infants would acquire golden complexions.

Inevitably, because saffron was so valuable, its fragrance was thought to have an aphrodisiac effect on the senses of a lover. Ayurveda uses small quantities of saffron in mixtures that are drunk to tone the uterus after childbirth and to regulate gynecological disorders, as well as for fevers, spasmodic coughs, and asthma. Saffron is also thought to be effective in improving vision and for curing melancholia.

Ayurveda considers the gloom-dispersing property of saffron to be so potent in restoring animal spirits that it even recommends infusing a few threads of saffron in drinking water to be given "to caged birds when they are molting or otherwise sickly."

57
Betel Leaf

(*Piper betle*)
Family: Piperaceae
Sanskrit name: Tambula
Hindi name: Pan

❧

At first too shy to approach the prince directly, Princess Kadambari was persuaded to honor her guest. She stretched out her hand. She placed the betel leaf in his. She offered the leaf as though she offered her heart.

Bānabhatta (seventh century A.D.),
Kadambari

Chew betel leaf, then go view yourself in a silver mirror before joining your friends.

Kama Sutra (circa fifth century A.D.)

Betel leaves chewed with areca nut, cloves, etcetera prevent halitosis.

Treatise of Charaka (first century A.D.)

This breath freshener, usually taken with areca nut and burnt lime paste, produces a deep red color used by Indians since earliest times to redden the lips. Those who can afford to do so, increase the fragrance of their betel leaf or pan by such additional aromatics as cloves, cardamoms, nutmegs, camphor, and other breath sweeteners.

According to Susruta, the great Ayurvedic surgeon of the fourth century A.D., the betel leaf is "aromatic, stimulant, carminative, astringent, aphrodisiac, and antiseptic."

The claims for the aphrodisiac qualities of the betel may be due to the alkaloid arakene, present in the leaf, which has properties allied to cocaine. Although the quantity present in betel leaf is considered much lower than that of cocaine, betel leaf is nonetheless an ancient addiction among Indians, who view it less as a stimulant than as a digestive: chewing betel leaf causes copious salivation, which assists in stimulating the gastric juices.

The delicate betel creeper grows in the hotter regions of India and must be nurtured with great care. But this care is bestowed most willingly on the vine by India's cultivators, since the pleasure which the betel leaf gives is so great that Indian mythology says even gods and goddesses long for it. Apparently the betel vine does not grow in heaven, so Hindus often place a betel leaf in the mouth of a corpse in order that the dead person can enjoy a last moment of pleasure before joining the gods.

58
True Indigo

(*Indigofera tinctoria*)
Family: Fabaceae
Sanskrit name: Nili
Hindi name: Neel

Indigo is a color most esteemed in India; out of India it comes; whereupon it took the name; and it is nothing else but a slimy mud that clings to the foam that gathers about cane and reeds; while it is panned it looks black; but when dissolved it yields an astonishingly lovely mixture of purple and azure.

In physic, there is use of this Indigo; for it assuages swellings that stretch the skin.

Pliny (A.D. 70)

*I*ndigo, a latin term for the greatest Indian dye, means the color of India, a color much in demand by the nobles of the Roman Empire.

In the navigational texts called the Periplus, compiled by an anonymous Greek sailor in the first century A.D., indigo is mentioned as having been a popular export from India to Egypt, and Sir John Gardner Wilkinson notes in his book *Ancient Egypt* (1878) that "the dye was used in Egyptian mummy cloths."

In the fifteenth century Thomas Malory described one of the knights of the Round Table appearing at King Arthur's court with no coat of arms blazoned on his armor, "only the colour of Ind."

The seventeenth-century French traveler Tavernier recorded the result of an experiment with the color while traveling through India: "One morning I placed an egg among those who sift indigo. And when I broke it in the evening, it was deep blue within." Because it cannot be washed out—hence its popularity as a dye for blue jeans—the color indigo represents knowledge or wisdom in Indian philosophy.

The indigo plant is mentioned in Indian scriptures as early as 300 B.C., and the wide variety of colors which can be obtained from the many species of this tall-standing shrub, often grown as a hedge around Indian houses, range from being likened to the reflection of the sky in water to the deep midnight blue which verges on black which is the divine color of Vishnu the Preserver.

As a cosmetic, indigo is used to make the hair dye most commonly used by Indians suffering from premature grayness, merging its own colors easily into the black which is the natural hair color of virtually every Indian. Indigo leaf extract is blended into various herbal oils and rubbed into the scalp to prevent hair loss after childbirth or a serious illness, or to inhibit premature balding, as the plant is thought to have properties that strengthen the roots of hair.

Ayurvedic medicine recommends applying the dye to soothe burns, scalds, and insect stings, as it is antiseptic and anti-inflammatory. But it also ascribes to this plant a medicinal property which can cure leucoderma, the large patches of white skin which appear with sudden and inexplicable loss of pigmentation and which are thought to be so disfiguring the condition is called in India "White Leprosy."

In one of the earliest Indian scriptures, the Yajurveda, this power is invoked with the prayer:

O Indigo, your mother the soil
Is black.
Your father, the seed
is black.
You, who inherit blackness,
Render me black and beautiful as well.
Remove my pale spots,
My graying hair,
My emblems of
White leprosy.

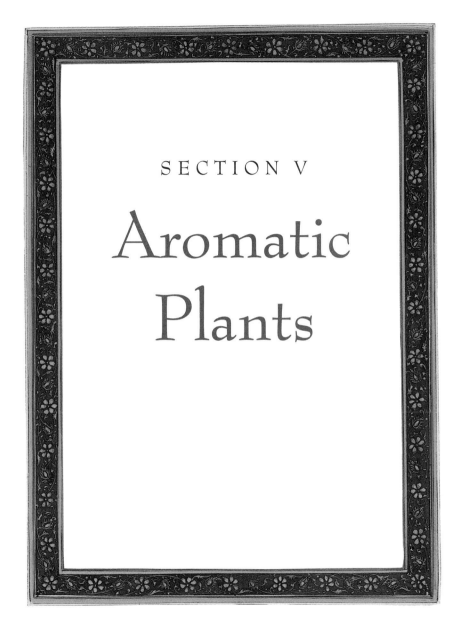

SECTION V

Aromatic Plants

AROMATIC PLANTS

The Charaka treatise emphasizes that the senses must be healthy if humans are to experience true well-being, and because Ayurveda considers the human body both in its totality as well as in its relation to nature, the garden and its flowers are essential to Ayurvedic science.

The most obvious sensory satisfaction provided by aromatic plants is the olfactory pleasure they give to human beings, and perfumery is one of India's most ancient and venerated crafts, integrated into India's daily life. Scented plants are used to celebrate every aspect of Indian culture, from the ritual to the culinary, from the celibate to the erotic. Because Indians do not distil perfume but extract it by causing it to be absorbed into various oils, in India to make a separation between perfumes, cosmetics, and condiments is not only extremely difficult but even illogical. And Ayurvedic science has gone even further, explaining the medicinal properties of many of these perfumes and aromatics.

For instance, certain aromatic gums and flowers are made into the incenses that are burned before family altars during morning and evening devotions. But one of the rules of hygiene created by Ayurveda requires the fumigation of chambers with incense, morning and evening, as a disinfectant, and against insects. The beautiful jasmine, with its elegant perfume and its pale flowers that blossom after dark soothing the eyes, is praised by Ayurveda for the jasmine juice which cures eye inflammation.

Scented flowers in India have always been strung into garlands or worn to decorate the hair. Ayurveda has examined the flowers which give Indians such pleasure and identified in their essential oils drugs capable of curing headaches, even migraines. Scented leaves with evocative folk names like "Protector of Children" are tested and discovered to contain properties that can lower a child's temperature or relieve his gastric problems.

The beauty of flowers and plants, especially scented plants, is considered by Ayurvedic psychiatrists to have a tranquilizing effect on those suffering from mental agitations. A classical Ayurvedic medical text specifically recommends that patients suffering from manic tendencies visit gardens with scented flowers, as an antidote to their mental propensities. "Among the cures for those of an overenergetic or fiery temperament is a visit to a pleasure garden. . . . They should scent themselves and enjoy the cool breeze."

Susruta, the great Ayurvedic surgeon of the fourth century A.D., observes in his treatise, "One in whom the physiological activities . . . are normal, and whose mind, spirit, and senses are in a tranquil condition, is considered healthy."

Over the centuries, Ayurvedic physicians have noticed that many plants grown by Ayurveda for medicinal purposes are also fragrant and ornamental. These physicians have encouraged their patients to grow such plants in their own gardens, not just as a pharmacopoeia or as pleasure to the senses. According to Ayurveda, growing these plants encourages people to tend nature rather than destroy it, increasing their consciousness of the daily and seasonal changes that affect mankind. The garden and the awareness of it provides medicine to both the body and its senses as well as to the spirit, and produces "that tranquil state" without which no person is truly healthy.

59

Jasmine

(*Jasminum grandiflorum*)
Family: Oleaceae
Sanskrit name: Jati
Hindi name: Mogra

You are the forest.
You are all the great trees.

O Lord White As Jasmine,
filling and filled by all.
Why don't you show me your face?
Mahadeviyakka, *Hymn to Siva*
(twelfth century A.D.)

The jasmine is the great summer flower of India, grown by verandahs or alongside garden walks where its white blossoms and delicate perfume can be enjoyed at night after the sun's heat has diminished. Jasmine buds and flowers are worn as scented ornaments—in the hair, as fragile garlands around the throat, through pierced earlobes, as bracelets circling the wrist. In many parts of India these strings of flowers are bound in plantain fiber when their buds are still tight so that they slowly open through the evening, keeping their light fragrance instead of producing the heavy scent that exudes from wilting jasmine flowers.

Indian women are partial to highly scented fragrances, and the oil pressed from jasmine flowers is a favorite Indian scent worn throughout the year, not just in summer. But this large twining shrub native to the northern Himalayas has provided Indians with cures as well as sensual pleasure.

Indian medicine uses twelve species of jasmine. The entire plant is used for a variety of Ayurvedic prescriptions. The juice pressed from jasmine leaves is used to remove corns. An infusion made from even a single jasmine flower will noticeably cool inflamed and bloodshot eyes. The leaves are used to make a gargle for mouth ulcers or other eruptions in the mouth.

The whole plant is considered effective in expelling worms, in regulating menstrual flow, and in helping to clear the kidneys of waste. Fresh jasmine flowers and jasmine oil are applied externally as cures for sores, especially in the case of abscesses, while jasmine-root extract is soaked in water and used as an eyewash.

60
Fragrant Screw Pine

(*Pandanus odoratissimus*)
Family: Pandanaceae
Sanskrit name: Ketaki
Hindi name: Kevda

Musk has the defect of being dry; this [the screw pine] may be called moist musk. It has a very agreeable scent . . . from the center of the flower comes the excellent perfume.

Moghul emperor Bābur,
Bābur-nameh (1525)

The perfume which the first Moghul emperor calls "excellent" is a bittersweet scent used by Indians to flavor food, as medicine, and to make perfume. In India the flower is so famous for its fragrance that the tree is not planted near a house for fear of snakes, which are reputed to be attracted by its perfume, which the fastidious Moghul emperors considered to be one of the finest scents India offered.

This small tree gains its English name from the spines which form a screw pattern on its leaves. Within the inner leaves grows the flower from which the screw pine draws its appellation "fragrant," although the spiny leaves are also aromatic. A perfumed oil and a fragrant attar are both extracted from the flower, and both used as medicines as well as scents.

Ayurvedic science finds the medicinal action of the essential oil yielded by the screw pine's highly scented flowers to be useful in headaches, earaches, and as a liniment for rheumatic pains. The distilled water made from the flowers is used for inducing perspiration. It is also prescribed as a stimulant and an antispasmodic.

The flowers themselves are powdered and included in medicines, which are either sniffed like snuff or smoked for asthma and other bronchial infections. And the root is administered in a milk preparation to prevent threatened abortion in pregnant women.

61
Bakula

(*Mimusops elengi*)
Family: Sapotaceae
Sanskrit name: Bakula
Hindi name: Bakula

I was in the courtyard beneath a young bakula tree so heavy with clusters of buds that bees swarmed thickly around its wine sweet perfume and the fallen flowers were in such great heaps I began to amuse myself weaving these into an intricate garland.

Bhavabhūti (eighth century A.D.),
Malati Madhavam

Like so many tropical scents, the fragrance exuded by the tiny flowers of the towering bakula tree is overpowering, with a distinctive and heady bouquet that lingers in the air, so strong it almost anesthetizes the senses. Perhaps it is fortunate that the bakula flowers only open after dark, beginning to scent at twilight, then throwing out their full fragrance into the night until dawn, when they fall from the tree onto the ground and are often collected by devotees and offered at temples.

Because the tree is so ornamental, with its flat leaves green on top and pale below and its creamy white star-shaped flowers, the bakula is often planted in Indian gardens, and Indians take much pleasure in coming out in the morning to collect the scented bakula blossoms strewn over their lawns.

The bakula also produces a berrylike fruit, which turns yellow when ripe. The pulp is given to patients suffering from stomach upsets, but the unripe berry is considered a useful masticatory, and is also used as an infusion to provide a general health tonic.

The flowers, fruit, and bark of the bakula are all astringent, and they are used as elements in an Ayurvedic lotion for wounds and ulcers. The bark, which is powdered and made into a gargle for infected mouth and gums, is one of the main ingredients in an Ayurvedic tooth powder recommended for patients with spongy gums.

62
Nutmeg

(*Myristica fragrans*)
Family: Myristicaceae
Sanskrit name: Jatiphala
Hindi name: Jaiphal

*Robed like a passionate girl
diffusing the fragrance
of flowering nutmeg.*
Bhartrhari, *Satakatraya*
(seventh century A.D.)

᠁

Nutmeg and mace come from the same tree, mace being the outer part of the fruit and nutmeg the kernel or seed, which is dried for several weeks on gratings over a slow charcoal fire until it is sufficiently cured to be insect repellant. When thoroughly dried nutmegs have a delightful fragrance and a very bitter warm taste.

Powdered nutmeg produces a strongly scented oil which is used in massage oils and perfumes, valued not just for their fragrance but also because ground nutmeg has been identified by Ayurvedic medicine as excellent for the maintenance of healthy skin and the prevention of scar formation. It is even used to cure mild cases of ringworm, a skin disease despite its name, and added to hair pomades to stimulate hair growth.

Since excessive doses of nutmeg, a narcotic, taken internally are traditionally thought to be capable of bringing on delirium or convulsions, Charaka recommends the sole use of nutmeg as a medicine for external applications only. But used in small amounts, powdered nutmeg forms one of the constituents of many Ayurvedic prescriptions for nausea, dysentery, insomnia, even delirium tremens, as well as smoker's cough and other bronchial irritations.

Nutmeg also provides a spice highly valued by Indians for the flavor and aroma it imparts to food. Similar to clove or Indian cinnamon, a pinch of nutmeg powder is often used to scent Indian puddings and sweets.

63
Clove

(*Syzygium aromaticum*)
Family: Myrtaceae
Sanskrit name: Lavanga
Hindi name: Long

Come, bridegroom, come.
I'll give your horse grain
And offer your companions cloves.
Come. Drink bhang to your heart's content.
Chew cloves and betel nut at my home.

from a traditional folk song of Rajasthan

❧

The fragrant clove, today so mundanely associated with the clove oil used as a remedy for toothaches, is one of the spices over which the nations of Europe went to war during the sixteenth and seventeenth centuries. Marco Polo numbered cloves among the most valuable treasures he brought back to Europe from his travels, and for several centuries they were such an expensive commodity in the West that the Portuguese, then the Dutch, then the French fought to control the trade in cloves, on occasion even destroying all the clove trees cultivated by Eastern farmers rather than letting them fall into the hands of their European enemies.

Such behavior would have astonished the peasants of Rajasthan, who found cloves desirable but commonplace.

A small evergreen tree, the entire clove plant is highly aromatic but the clove itself is the calyx of the flower picked in bud and dried in the sun. The most aromatic part of the tree, the clove, is one of the spices used sparingly in Indian rices and curries, to add a distinctive aroma to the dish.

The pungent, aromatic clove is widely used by Indians as a mouth freshener, and Charaka notes its value as an antiseptic for inflammations of the mouth and throat, as well as its capacity to cure halitosis both by its scent and its digestive action, since bad breath is often caused by poor digestion. Later, Ayurvedic physicians called the clove the most stimulating and carminative of all aromatics. The oil is a strong antiseptic and germicide, although its potency as a local anesthetic, as in cases of toothache, is quite feeble.

64 ☙ Camphor

(*Cinnamomum camphora*)
Family: Lauraceae
Sanskrit name: Karpuram
Hindi name: Kapur

One hundred horsemen and upwards may rest in the shade of a single tree. Some say snakes wind themselves around these trees in summer because they are especially cool, seeing which, men mark the trees with arrows and return to collect the camphor in winter; others say the trees are especially favored by leopards.

The camphor crystallizing on the inside of the tree looks like salt; on its outside, like resin; and it often runs onto the ground where it solidifies. . . . According to some books it is white as snow, and this is true. I have seen it.

Abul Fazl Allami, *Chronicles of the Emperor Akbar* (sixteenth century A.D.)

The evergreen camphor tree grows to a great size and with its many branches and small white clusters of flowers is reminiscent of the linden trees of Europe. The white substance extracted from its wood, the camphor, is so pure that it is burned as an incense on its own—a lump of camphor placed on a green leaf in front of an idol sending up a clear blue flame as it releases its powerful aroma.

Most parts of the camphor tree can be used to distil an oil that is valued for its medicinal purposes, as well as the white crystalline substance, known as camphor, which has a very distinctive and penetrating fragrance.

Because the strong scent of camphor protects animal substances from insects, it is used in Indian kitchens, wherever there are drains or running water from which cockroaches might appear. It is also the most popular insecticide for protecting clothing against moths, and papers against termites. As an antiseptic, camphor is used to disinfect rooms during epidemics. The properties of camphor's scent are so widely acknowledged that it is now favored all over the world for constructing cabinets containing natural history displays, as a means of protecting the dead exhibits from the attentions of their living brethren.

While the aroma is highly prized by Indians, it is more associated with medicine than with perfume. Most commonly used in vapors and liniments for colds, chills, and inflammatory conditions, camphor is slightly cold to the touch.

Camphor is used in Ayurveda locally, to numb the peripheral sensory nerves and as a counterirritant in rheumatisms and sprains and inflammatory conditions. Physicians prescribe camphor internally for its calming influence in hysteria, neuralgia, and other nervous ailments, and it is sometimes used in cases of heart failure. But Ayurvedic science stresses that camphor is very acrid and taken in large doses, highly poisonous.

65
Golden Champa

(*Michelia champaca*)
Family: Magnoliaceae
Sanskrit name: Champaka
Hindi name: Champa

Just as a fabric obtains fragrance from its association with sweet-scented champa flowers, so does the spirit from its association with the intellect.

Indian philosophical treatise
(circa A.D. 320, Gupta Period)

The golden champa, with its yellow scented flowers, is a tree often mentioned in tribal folk tales. Over and over again the myths of the forest tribals teach respect for nature by deifying plants or having human beings transformed into plants, a transformation which is usually linked to good fortune. In tribal folklore the golden champa is an incarnation of the Goddess of Wealth, and one of the stories tells of a court minister's virtuous daughter, who is transformed into a champa tree bearing not yellow flowers but flowers of solid gold.

Although the golden champa is cultivated for its fragrant flowers, which are used in the preparation of perfumes and hair oils, its fresh flowers are one of the favorite hair ornaments of Indian women. In south India where the tree grows abundantly, women wear a closed golden champa in their long hair, allowing their body heat to cause the flower to open into a scented blossom as the evening progresses. The highly scented blossoms are also a favorite offering to the gods at Hindu temples, and these trees are often to be found growing in temple precincts.

A scented oil extracted from the blossoms of the golden champa is applied to the temples to relieve vertigo, and considered useful as a liniment for relieving pain from headaches, rheumatism, and gout, as well as for relieving burning sensations in a variety of skin diseases ranging from allergic disorders to sores.

Ayurveda uses the bark and the fruit of the golden champa, as well as the scented flowers, in its medicines. A bark concoction is prescribed for gastritis and urinary problems; the champa's young leaves are crushed in water to make a cooling antiseptic lotion used as eyedrops; the leaves and flowers are applied to the head to soothe patients suffering from anemea delirium, and manic symptoms; the seeds are known to be effective in expelling intestinal worms.

The Indian forest tribals consider the various parts of the golden champa useful for a wide range of illnesses, including ulcers, dysentery, bronchitis, heavy menstrual flow, childbirth fevers, and spermatorrhea. Most interestingly, a large part of India's tribal population traditionally uses the stem bark of the golden champa as a contraceptive agent.

66
Aloeswood

(*Aquilaria agallocha*)
Family: Thymelaeaceae
Sanskrit name: Agaru
Hindi name: Agar

Aloeswood is often used in compound perfumes. When eaten, it is exhilarating. It is generally employed in incense. The better qualities, powdered, are used for rubbing into the skin and clothes.

Ain-i-Akbari (1595), the chronicles of the reign
of the Great Moghul, Emperor Akbar

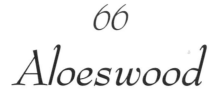

This large evergreen tree with its slightly leathery leaves and clusters of tiny white flowers, found on the foothills of the Himalayan mountains, provides the basis for Indian incense. In fact its very name in Hindi, *agar*, forms the Indian word for incense—*agarbati*, or "lighted aloeswood." Under certain conditions which man has not been able to duplicate or even to assess, a change takes place in both the trunk and branches and the wood becomes gorged with a dark, resinous, aromatic juice. Unfortunately, no external mark indicates which trees are secreting the valuable aloe resin, used from ancient times, in both India and China, for the making of incense, perfumes, and medicine.

The incense offered at temples or ceremonial rituals usually includes other substances, but aloeswood incense is offered in devotions, which take place in the house, before family altars, and it is the scent which most Indians associate with home and the comforts of a family life. Even Indians who do not use the incense for ritual purposes use it as a fumigant in the evenings when mosquitoes appear. The Indian twilight is marked with clouds of aloe incense as braziers filled with chips of smoking aloeswood are swung in room after room of the house and the doors closed, to kill any mosquitoes and insects in the chambers.

Fortunately, the other wood of this tree, which is so often felled without certainty of finding any aromatic incense, is used by Ayurvedic medicine. Charaka indicates aloeswood can be powdered to provide external and internal prescriptions in cases of poisoning and fever.

Because of its astringent nature, the powdered wood of the aloe tree provides an effective skin tonic and is recommended by Ayurvedic physicians as an application for restoring pigment in leucoderma. Also, powdered aloeswood provides an antiseptic so gentle it is used for ear and eye infections as well as on open wounds.

67
Kadamba

(*Anthocephalus cadamba*)
Family: Rubiaceae
Sanskrit name: Kadamba
Hindi name: Kadam

Instructions on propitiating the God of Love:

Repeat the prayer 10,000 times as counted on a garland of kadamba blossoms . . . a single flower to be given to the lady.

Kalyanamalla, *Ananga Ranga*
(circa fifteenth century A.D.)

The honey-colored flowers of the kadamba tree only open after dark to produce the wine-rich scent that is extracted into a perfumed oil much loved in India. The flower itself, a sphere made of pale golden florettes, is used as mystic symbol by worshippers of the Goddess, and the name of the tree is synonymous with wine, after a legend that says an evil demon became so intoxicated by the fragrant wine dripping from the kadamba's flowers that he was unable to wreak destruction. Although the kadamba flowers produce no wine, a mild spirit can be distilled from the petals.

The most widespread legends concerning the kadamba tree spring from the kadamba's association with the cowherd god, Krishna. He is said to have stood in its shade when playing his flute, and to have climbed its branches when he stole the clothes of a group of bathing maidens.

Krishna is the god most Indians associate with children, and many of the Krishna legends tell of his antics as a child, so perhaps it is no accident that this tree so strongly associated with him should carry the popular name "Protector of Children."

The fruit of the kadamba tree is about the size of an orange with fleshy orange pulp. The squeezed fruit juice is mixed with cuminseed and sugar and given to children for gastric irritability, and the whole fruit is useful when children are running high temperatures because it cools and quenches thirst.

The fresh juice of the kadamba bark is applied to the heads of newborn infants when the fontanel sinks, and the juice of the kadamba fruit is used by the entire family as a health tonic and to allay stomach disorders.

68
Vetiver

(*Vetiveria zizanioides*)
Family: Gramineae
Sanskrit name: Ushira
Hindi name: Khas

Vetiver blinds, that lend
to burning summer noons
the scented chill
of winter nights.
Bihari (1595–1664),
The Satasai

⊰⊱

Vetiver is the scent which India associates with summer, especially the burning noons of northern India when the temperature rises to 114° F. and just the heat of the wind on the skin can lead to dehydration. This is the time when no Indian will venture out of doors, abandoning the empty streets to Noël Coward's mad dogs and Englishmen. Better to remain indoors, the windows of the houses darkened with heavy blinds woven from the wiry, fibrous roots of vetiver—a densely tufted perennial grass that grows wild in the hotter regions of India. The vetiver blinds are continually doused with water throughout the day, turning the very wind that can dehydrate a person walking in the sun into a scented cooling breeze, which passes through the soaked vetiver releasing a bittersweet aroma. Ayurveda recommends this scent for heatstroke, headaches, and to delay senile decay; it's the scent that Indian poets refer to as the smell of the first monsoon shower on parched soil, the perfume of a rejuvenated earth.

The common Western name of this grass comes from its Tamil name, *vettiver*, literally "hatcheted up," an exact description of how the spongy roots, so valued for their aroma, are collected. Although vetiver on its own is a favorite perfume not just in India but around the world, the essential oil taken from these roots when they are soaked in water is not very volatile, so it is often used as a fixative for other perfumes. The extreme purity of the oil makes it safe for eating, and it is used in India to flavor summer sherbets, ice creams, and digestives—another example of how Ayurvedic knowledge overlaps in India with traditional practice, since Ayurveda recommends vetiver-root infusions to reduce thirst, burning micturition, and fevers.

Ayurvedic medicine also recommends applying a paste made from vetiver root to the skin to bring down body temperature in cases of fever or heat stroke, and rubbing a liniment made from vetiver's essential oil to relieve rheumatic pains.

69 ⚜ Hundred Leaf Rose

(*Rosa centifolia*)
Family: Rosaceae
Sanskrit name: Shatapatri
Hindi name: Gulab

*His eyes are those of a woman
But he uses the language of men.*

Let's take him to a garden and watch.

*For a woman eats the fruit that falls from the
  trees
But a man, who is a man, plucks the rose.*
  "Ballad of Sajna," folk song from Rajasthan

*I*ndia has many roses, both wild and cultivated. In the fourteenth century, a Persian traveler touring Gujarat on the western coast of India, counted over seventy different species of rose cultivated by the inhabitants in their gardens, and at the begining of the seventeenth century, the Moghul emperor, Jahāngīr, noted in his memoirs that India possessed every sort of rose, particularly the musk and the damask.

But the hundred leaf rose, or as it is more commonly known, the cabbage rose, produces both the famous Indian attar of roses which is used as perfume and for scenting soaps and bath oils, as well as the drug extracts which are official in the Indian pharmacopoeia.

Distilled cabbage rose water is used as a vehicle for eye lotions and eyewashes. Its rose hips are dried and made into tisanes for children with stomach disorders, and are also considered a cardiotonic for adults. Its petals are used by Ayurvedic medicine to make a syrup which acts as a gentle laxative.

Roses play a part in many Indian ceremonials, as the petals easily impart their scent to water. Rose water is sprinkled on guests when they enter a marriage pavilion, to scent them and to cool them with its astringent quality. It is given to elders to wash their hands as a gesture of respect. It is sprinkled in rooms to freshen the air and give the room a sweet smell. Indian rulers and courts traditionally used rose water to scent their audience halls.

Rose petals, rose water, and rose oil are also used in Indo-Islamic cuisine, to flavor and scent sweet dishes and summer sherbets.

70
Sandalwood

(Santalam album)
Family: Santalaceae
Sanskrit name: Chandana
Hindi name: Safed Chandan

The rocky slopes were cooled by breezes fragrant with the scent of crushed sandalwood uprooted by playful elephants, and in the dense forests interlaced with creepers, nymphs gathered.

Subandhu, *Vasavadatta*,
a novel (seventh century A.D.)

⁂

*I*n the 1920s a group of British engineers laying a railway track near the holy city of Varanasi unearthed an alabaster casket filled with sandalwood paste. The alabaster casket was dated by archaeologists as having been made around A.D. 400, indicating that this scented Indian wood which is used to make perfumes, incenses, face masks, and soaps all over contemporary India was highly prized in early classical India as well. Of course, Indian literature and mythology are replete with references to sandalwood, especially as an erotic perfume and paste.

This small tree, which seldom grows higher than twenty feet and which is valued for the essential oil santalol, yielded only by its heart wood and roots, is depicted in Indian religious mythology as surrounded by snakes, their venom reduced by the tree's cooling fragrance. Because the scent-yielding wood is in the center of the trunk or underground, it is a favorite wood for Hindu religious rituals, in which no offering, no matter how sweet its perfume, can be made to the sacred fire if it has been urinated on by any animal. Devotees often rub the foreheads of religious idols with sandalwood paste, and it is one of the woods placed on a Hindu's funeral pyre, probably to overcome the smell.

Sandalwood is ground into a paste and worn on the forehead between the eyebrows as a caste mark by followers of the gods Vishnu and Shiva. Interestingly, Ayurveda says there is a central nerve or node of nerves where these marks are applied so the application of cooling sandalwood at this spot serves to tranquilize a believer as well as indicating his or her religious preference.

All Indians value this scented wood, which has always provided so many of their favorite unguents, and which is immune to the deprecations of woodworm and white ants, but Ayurvedic medicine uses it for providing a paste that is not just cooling and antiseptic but also anti-inflammatory and styptic, capable of stopping local bleeding in cuts and other wounds.

Taken in a drink, powdered sandalwood is used to relieve burning sensations in urinary disorders or cases of ulcers. Applied as a paste, it maintains skin health throughout the summer months and is described by Ayurveda as a certain cure for heat rashes.

Ayurvedic Health Centers in India

1. A & U Tibbia College Hospital, Karol Bagh, Delhi.
2. Gujaret Ayurveda University, Jamnager, Gujarat.
3. Akhandananda Ayurvedic Hospital, Ahmedabad, Gujarat.
4. Rohtak Ayurvedic College Hospital, Rohtak, Haryana.
5. Government Ayurvedic College Hospital, Kurukshetra, Haryana.
6. Government Ayurvedic Hospital, Mysore, Karnataka.
7. Government Ayurvedic College Hospital, Thiruvananthapuram, Kerala.
8. Government Ayurvedic College Hospital, Thripunithura, Kerala.
9. Arya Vaidya Shala, Kottakkal, Kerala.
10. R. R. A. Podar Ayurvedic Hospital, Worli, Bombay, Maharashtra.
11. Changani Ayurvedic Hospital, Nagpur, Maharashtra.
12. Government Ayurvedic College Hospital, Puri, Orissa.
13. Government Ayurvedic Hospital, Patiala, Punjab.
14. National Institute of Ayurveda, Amer Road, Jaipur, Rajasthan.
15. Government Ayurvedic College Hospital, Udaipur, Rajasthan.
16. Indian Medicine Practitioners Cooperative Pharmacy and Stores Ltd. Hospital, Lattice Bridge Road, Adyar, Madras, Tamil Nadu.
17. Government Ayurvedic College Hospital, Lucknow, Uttar Pradesh.

Ayurvedic Health Centers in the United States

1. The Institute for Human Potential and Mind Body Medicine
   (Deepak Chopra, Executive Director)
   8010 Frost Street, Suite 30Q, San Diego, CA 92123, (619) 541-6730
2. The Ayurvedic Institute
   P.O. Box 23445, Albuquerque, NM 87192, (505) 291-9698
3. The Center for Perfect Health
   Oxnard, CA, (805) 485-2883
4. The Raj
   24th Street NW, Fairfield, IA 52556, (800) 248-9050
5. Lotus Ayurvedic Center
   1505 42nd Avenue, Suite 19, Capitola, CA 95010, (408) 479-1667

The Artists

When I decided to commission original paintings to illustrate the plants of the Ayurveda, I approached my friend and colleague, the artist **Bannu**, with whom I had collaborated on my first book, *A Second Paradise*.

A tall man in his forties, Bannu lives in the oldest part of Jaipur City in a narrow four-storeyed house which his family has occupied for almost two centuries. Bannu's family have been the hereditary painters to the Maharajas of Jaipur, and Bannu still possesses many sketches and paintings by his artistic forebears in the style known as the Jaipur School of miniature painting, famous for its moustachioed men and the voluptuous women, which Bannu enjoys painting himself.

Bannu's studio is reached by climbing a flight of steep stone stairs leading to a wooden archway that opens onto an enclosed courtyard overlooked by the numerous whitewashed balconies of his house. Beyond the archway is Bannu's studio, which also doubles as living room where he receives his guests. The carpets on the floor are covered with white sheets. Bannu sits cross-legged on the floor, his back resting against bolster cushions, his wooden drawing board with its sheet of handmade paper supported on one knee. In front of him is a row of clamshells containing different colors that Bannu has himself painstakingly ground together in a mortar and pestle from ancestral recipes to produce the pigments he needs—colors which he makes from stones such as malachite, lapis lazuli, turquoise; from plants such as lime, kamila, madder, indigo; and from a variety of mineral and animal substances. His paintbrushes, like his colors, are also made according to his own specifications. One brush is even made from the single hair of a squirrel's tail, a hair so fine it allows him to paint each detail of a man's beard.

Such exquisite detail is characteristic of miniature painting. The art of miniature painting was introduced to India by the Moghul emperors, and was greatly influenced by Persian courtly art. As in Persia, Indian miniature paintings were often pasted into the albums of the privileged, on the opposing page to a written text. But the lighter hues of the Persian palette acquired in India the stronger, darker colors of the Indian palette, and Indian mythology and nature were added to its subject matter. This indigenous form of miniature painting blossomed in the Indian kingdoms, some of the most famous and accomplished artists belonging to the Jaipur School, known for the sensuality of its pictures.

When I asked Bannu if he would be prepared to execute botanical illustrations, he readily agreed, eager to see how the plants which form the thick background of vegetation in most miniatures would look when enlarged individually. I showed him the list of Ayurvedic plants I had chosen and Bannu pointed out that he, like any other Indian, was already familiar with most of them. His wife used some plants in her kitchen and stored others in the family medicine chest; some were used in the family's religious rituals, some by the women of the house for cosmetics and perfumes, still others were plants from which he extracted his own paints. Bannu also told me that his grandfather, who had been his art teacher, had sent him to the fields outside the city to gather plants as subjects for his lessons. As if to prove his familiarity with them, a dried specimen of each plant Bannu had painted—henna, vetiver, turmeric—accompanied his completed paintings.

Because I wanted the book to reflect a cross section of Indian art, I asked eight artists to illustrate the plants of the Ayurveda, but Jaipur is today such a center for miniature paintings that the artist **Ghanshyam Nimbark**, is also from Jaipur City. In his early thirties, Ghanshyam has already gained a considerable reputation for his imaginative and creative renderings of Indian miniatures. His illustrations try to fuse the subject with his art, and I was fascinated to learn that he had insisted on using true indigo colors for his painting of the indigo plant. In his rendition of a group of people celebrating the festival of color, he made his paints from the flowers of the Flame-of-the-Forest tree, the same flowers which are dried and powdered to make the colors flung about with such abandon during the festival.

A few years ago, while researching my second book, *A Desert Kingdom*, I spent some time in the erstwhile kingdom of Bikaner which lies on the edge of the Thar Desert. Inside the imposing walls of Bikaner Fort I saw exquisitely painted halls and chambers executed in the local miniature style. **Mahaveer Swami**, once a student under Bannu, lives in Bikaner City, the capital of this desert kingdom. Mahaveer now has pupils of his own, who come to learn the Bikaner tradition of using subtle colors to lend an almost mysterious quality to a picture, as can be seen in Mahaveer's illustrations of the banyan tree or the holy basil. Mahaveer was particularly pleased to paint plants from the Ayurveda. He told me his father, also a miniature artist and his first teacher, had been forced to stop painting when the kingdom of Bikaner was merged into the Indian republic in 1949. Unable to find a patron to take the place of his royal patrons, Mahaveer's father had taken a job with an Ayurvedic physician: the doctor was able to use the artist's skill and knowledge in finding and grinding plants.

Because of his father's experience, Mahaveer Swami is himself very interested in plants, and when his young cousin, **Raju Swami**, decided to become an artist, Mahaveer sent Raju into the inhospitable terrain outside Bikaner City to study and paint plants in their natural habitat. Raju, with all the spontaneity of a young man still in his early twenties, has now become something of an experimenter with plants and plant extracts. He asked me to sniff his completed painting of the garland of jasmine flowers, and was delighted that I found the scent of jasmine so strong. He had used the juice of jasmine flowers to shade the painted blossoms.

The artist **Kailash Chand Sharma** lives in Delhi, but he often visits his family home in a village on the foothills of the Himalayan mountains. Both he and his brother, also an artist, are adept at the Pahari, or mountain, School of art fostered by the courts and temples in this area. Pahari miniatures are known by their movement, their bright colors, and their strong evocation of changing seasons. All these characteristics are visible in Kailash Chand's illustrations, but he has added his own elaborate borders around the pictures, themselves illustrations of the plants. He was also surprisingly knowledgeable about the medicinal values of certain plants, particularly the Indian pennywort, which he had seen being collected from the water's edge as a child.

Two artists from south India, which has no tradition of miniature art, painted illustrations for this book. As they were both from coastal areas that had long been centers of international trade, their work also showed influences from outside India. But they were both familiar with painting plants.

K. K. Shreedhara is from a family of textile weavers who live near the great temple of Tanjore. From his childhood he watched his father design elaborate floral patterns for temple garments and hangings, and as an adult Shreedhara became equally adept at using flowers and plants for designs rendered on silks or carpets. But his botanical paintings freed him from the restrictions of traditional design, and I was interested to see the Chinese influence in his picture of the asparagus racemosus, or the Arab influence in his Indian bedellium set on the Arabian Sea bordering the desert region of Kutch, which he captures so unself-consciously, although he has never seen a desert.

The second artist from south India, **A. Ranjit**, was also influenced by the temple art of south India. The stone sculptures of Madurai and Meenakshi temples, the great bronzes of the Chola period, inspired him to become a sculptor. When he traveled across India to see the murals of Ajanta and Ellora he decided to attempt the miniature style of painting. Still, the strength of his earlier influences, as indeed the power of the monsoons in his own region, are obvious in such pictures as his illustration of the hogweed.

Banwari Lal Rajpoot lives in his ancestral home in Old Delhi, once the center of miniature painting during the Moghul Empire. As befits an imperial school of art, many Moghul miniatures were portraits, and Banwari Lal has been trained in the Moghul style. But he is not inflexible about following tradition. On the contrary, he used his skills as a miniature portraitist to produce an exquisite picture of a madder root. When I asked how he had painted a botanical picture in such detail, he replied that his long training in rendering each hair of a man's beard exactly had given him the skill to paint the root hairs of the madder plant. As a master artist, he also displayed the most charming modesty about his work, telling me that he flashed his pictures in front of young children rather as flash cards are used when children are learning to read. If the children immediately shouted out the name of the plant, he was reassured that he was painting it correctly, and when I told him that black pepper had been an important item in the European spice trade, he couldn't resist painting a Union Jack onto a ship in full sail.

Each of the eight artists who contributed their talents so enthusiastically to this book has won prestigious national awards in India. They have all exhibited their work both at home and abroad, in numerous European countries as well as in some Asian countries such as Japan. Their art illustrates how the plant knowledge of India and traditional Indian painting overlap, both part of a living culture which I hope will never become extinct.

Artists Index

Bannu:
- 10. Jamun
- 14. Asoka
- 21. Bauhinia
- 46. Mahua
- 47. Henna
- 53. Turmeric
- 63. Clove
- 68. Vetiver

Ghanshyam Nimbark:
- 8. Indian Hemp
- 25. Eclipta Alba
- 32. Cumin
- 51. Areca Nut Palm
- 55. Lime
- 57. Betel Leaf
- 58. True Indigo
- 61. Bakula

Mahaveer Swami:
- 1. Banyan
- 2. Lotus
- 3. Holy Basil
- 7. Ustram Bead
- 19. Chebulic Myrobalan
- 28. Arjun
- 30. Thorn Apple
- 52. Soap Nut

Raju Swami:
- 4. Flame-of-the-Forest
- 15. Castor
- 16. Indian Gentian
- 22. Swallowwort

- 24. Plantain
- 35. Mango
- 38. Cardamom
- 40. Eggplant
- 48. Sesame
- 50. Hibiscus
- 59. Jasmine
- 62. Nutmeg

Kailash Chand Sharma:
- Frontispiece, Plantain
- 5. Coconut
- 6. Bel
- 9. Sacred Fig
- 11. Margosa
- 12. Indian Pennywort
- 20. Emblic Myrobalan
- 23. Indian Laburnum
- 31. Winter Cherry
- 37. Palmyra
- 39. Indian Cassia Lignea
- 42. Tamarind
- 45. Cinnamon
- 54. Indian Kamila
- 64. Camphor
- 66. Aloeswood
- 67. Kadamba
- 69. Hundred Leaf Rose
- 70. Sandalwood

K. K. Shreedhara:
- 13. Asparagus Racemosus
- 18. Vasaka
- 29. Indian Bedellium

34. Coriander
41. Drumstick
44. Ginger

A. Ranjit:

26. Hogweed
49. Indian Sarsaparilla

Banwari Lal Rajpoot:

17. Liquorice

27. Indian Madder
33. Black Pepper
36. Bitter Gourd
43. Garlic
56. Saffron
60. Fragrant Screw Pine
65. Golden Champa

Plant Names

No.	English Name	Botanical Name	Family	Sanskrit Name	Hindi Name

SECTION 1—SACRED PLANTS

No.	English Name	Botanical Name	Family	Sanskrit Name	Hindi Name
1	Banyan	*Ficus bengalensis*	Moraceae	Nyagrodha	Bar
2	Lotus	*Nelumbo nucifera*	Nelumbonaceae	Padma	Kamal
3	Holy Basil	*Ocimum sanctum*	Labiatae	Tulasi	Tulasi
4	Flame-of-the-Forest	*Butea monosperma*	Papilionaceae	Palasha	Dhak
5	Coconut	*Cocos nucifera*	Palmaceae	Narikela	Nariyal
6	Bel	*Aegle marmelos*	Rutaceae	Bilva	Bel
7	Ustram Bead	*Elaeocarpus ganitrus*	Elaeocarpaceae	Rudraksha	Rudraksha
8	Indian Hemp	*Cannabis sativa*	Cannabinaceae	Vijaya	Bhang
9	Sacred Fig	*Ficus religiosa*	Moraceae	Ashvattha	Pipal
10	Jamun	*Syzygium cumini*	Myrtaceae	Jambu	Jamun
11	Margosa	*Azadirachta indica*	Meliaceae	Nimba	Neem

SECTION II—MEDICINAL PLANTS

No.	English Name	Botanical Name	Family	Sanskrit Name	Hindi Name
12	Indian Pennywort	*Centella asiatica*	Umbelliferae	Brahmi	Brahmi
13	Asparagus Racemosus	*Asparagus racemosus*	Liliaceae	Satavari	Satavar
14	Asoka	*Saraca asoca*	Caesalpinaceae	Ashoka	Ashok
15	Castor	*Ricinus communis*	Euphorbiaceae	Eranda	Rendi
16	Indian Gentian	*Andrographis paniculata*	Acanthaceae	Kalamegha	Kalmegh

No.	English Name	Botanical Name	Family	Sanskrit Name	Hindi Name
17	Liquorice	*Glycyrrhiza glabra*	Papilionaceae	Yastimadhu	Mulethi
18	Vasaka	*Adhatoda vasica*	Acanthaceae	Vasaka	Adusa
19	Chebulic Myrobalan	*Terminalia chebula*	Combretaceae	Haritaki	Harad
20	Emblic Myrobalan	*Emblica officinalis*	Euphorbiaceae	Amlaki	Amla
21	Bauhinia	*Bauhinia variegata*	Caesalpiniaceae	Kanchnara	Kachnar
22	Swallowwort	*Calotropis gigantea*	Asclepiadaceae	Arka	Aak
23	Indian Laburnum	*Cassia fistula*	Caesalpiniaceae	Aragvadha	Amaltas
24	Plantain	*Musa paradisiaca*	Musaceae	Kadali-phala	Kela
25	Eclipta Alba	*Eclipta alba*	Asteraceae	Bhringaraja	Bhangra
26	Hogweed	*Boerhaavia diffusa*	Nyctaginaceae	Punarnava	Gadahpurna
27	Indian Madder	*Rubia cordifolia*	Rubiaceae	Manjishtha	Manjith
28	Arjun	*Terminalia arjuna*	Combretaceae	Arjuna	Arjun
29	Indian Bedellium	*Commiphora mukul*	Burseraceae	Guggulu	Guggal
30	Thorn Apple	*Datura alba*	Solanaceae	Dhatura	Dhatura
31	Winter Cherry	*Withania somnifera*	Solanaceae	Ashvagandha	Asagandh

SECTION III—CULINARY PLANTS

No.	English Name	Botanical Name	Family	Sanskrit Name	Hindi Name
32	Cumin	*Cuminum cyminum*	Umbelliferae	Jiraka	Jeera
33	Black Pepper	*Piper nigrum*	Piperaceae	Marica	Kalimrich
34	Coriander	*Coriandrum sativum*	Umbelliferae	Dhanyaka	Dhaniya

No.	English Name	Botanical Name	Family	Sanskrit Name	Hindi Name
35	Mango	*Mangifera indica*	Anacardiaceae	Amra	Aam
36	Bitter Gourd	*Momordica charantia*	Cucurbitaceae	Karavela	Karela
37	Palmyra	*Borassus flabellifer*	Palmae	Tala	Tada
38	Cardamom	*Elettaria cardamomum*	Zingiberaceae	Ela	Ilaichi
39	Indian Cassia Lignea	*Cinnamomum tamala*	Lauraceae	Tamala Patra	Tejpatta
40	Eggplant	*Solanum melongena*	Solanaceae	Vrintaka	Baigun
41	Drumstick	*Moringa oleifera*	Moringaceae	Sigru	Sahajan
42	Tamarind	*Tamarindus indica*	Caesalpinaceae	Chincha	Imli
43	Garlic	*Allium sativum*	Aliaceae	Rasona	Lasan
44	Ginger	*Zingiber officinale*	Zingiberaceae	Shunthi	Adrak
45	Cinnamon	*Cinnamomum zeylanicum*	Lauraceae	Tvak	Dalchini
46	Mahua	*Madhuca longifolia*	Sapotaceae	Madhuka	Mahuva

SECTION IV—COSMETIC PLANTS

No.	English Name	Botanical Name	Family	Sanskrit Name	Hindi Name
47	Henna	*Lawsonia inermis*	Lythraceae	Madayantika	Mehndi
48	Sesame	*Sesamum indicum*	Pedaliaceae	Tila	Til
49	Indian Sarsaparilla	*Hemidesmus indicus*	Asclepiadaceae	Sariva	Anantmul
50	Hibiscus	*Hibiscus rosa-sinensis*	Malvaceae	Japakusuma	Gurhal
51	Areca Nut Palm	*Areca catechu*	Palmae	Puga	Supari

No.	English Name	Botanical Name	Family	Sanskrit Name	Hindi Name
52	Soap Nut	*Sapindus trifoliatus*	Sapindaceae	Aristaka	Ritha
53	Turmeric	*Curcuma longa*	Zingiberaceae	Haridra	Haldi
54	Indian Kamila	*Mallotus philippensis*	Euphorbiaceae	Kampillaka	Kampillaka
55	Lime	*Citrus medica*	Rutaceae	Nimbuka	Nimbu
56	Saffron	*Crocus sativus*	Iridaceae	Kumkuma	Kesar
57	Betel Leaf	*Piper betle*	Piperaceae	Tambula	Pan
58	True Indigo	*Indigofera tinctoria*	Fabaceae	Nili	Neel

SECTION V — AROMATIC PLANTS

No.	English Name	Botanical Name	Family	Sanskrit Name	Hindi Name
59	Jasmine	*Jasminum grandiflorum*	Oleaceae	Jati	Mogra
60	Fragrant Screw Pine	*Pandanus odoratissimus*	Pandanaceae	Ketaki	Kevda
61	Bakula	*Mimusops elengi*	Sapotaceae	Bakula	Bakula
62	Nutmeg	*Myristica fragrans*	Myristicaceae	Jatiphala	Jaiphal
63	Clove	*Syzygium aromaticum*	Myrtaceae	Lavanga	Long
64	Camphor	*Cinnamomum camphora*	Lauraceae	Karpuram	Kapur
65	Golden Champa	*Michelia champaca*	Magnoliaceae	Champaka	Champa
66	Aloeswood	*Aquilaria agallocha*	Thymelaeaceae	Agaru	Agar
67	Kadamba	*Anthocephalus cadamba*	Rubiaceae	Kadamba	Kadam
68	Vetiver	*Vetiveria zizanioides*	Gramineae	Ushira	Khas
69	Hundred Leaf Rose	*Rosa centifolia*	Rosaceae	Shatapatri	Gulab
70	Sandalwood	*Santalam album*	Santalaceae	Chandana	Safed Chandan

Bibliography

The Ain-i-Akbari, H. Blochmann, translator. Revised and edited by Lt. Col. D. C. Phillott. Published by Oriental Books, Reprint Corporation, New Delhi, 1977.

AMBASTA, S. P., editor-in-chief, *The Useful Plants of India*. Printed by Publications and Information Directorate, C.S.I.R., New Delhi, 1986.

ANDERSON, FRANK J., *An Illustrated History of the Herbals*. First edition printed 1912; published by Columbia University Press, New York, 1977.

ASHRAF, JAWEED, *Ethico-Cultural Dimensions of Man-Nature Relations: Ecology and Plant Domestication Under the Sultanate of Delhi*. Published by Indian Institute of Advanced Study, Simla, 1992.

ASHRAF, JAWEED, *Latin American Plants in Pre-Columbian Iconography, History and Culture of India*. Published by Indian Institute of Advanced Study, Simla, 1992.

AUBOYER, JEANNINE, *Daily Life in Ancient India*. Translated from French by Simon Watson Taylor. Printed by Asia Publishing House and Wiedenfeld & Nicholson, London, 1965.

BANERJEE S. C., *Flora and Fauna in Sanskrit Literature*. Published by B. Mitra Nayaprokash, Calcutta, 1980.

BASHAM, A. L., *The Wonder that Was India*. Published by Sidgwick & Jackson, London, 1985.

BIANCHINI, FRANCESCO and FRANCESCO CORBETTA, *Health Plants of the World*. Illustrated by Marilena Pistoia. English adaptation by M. A. Dejey. Published by Newsweek Books, New York, first edition 1977; third edition 1979.

BOR, N. L. and M. B. RAIZADA, *Some Beautiful Indian Climbers and Shrubs*. Published by Oxford University Press, Delhi, first edition 1954; revised edition 1982.

CHANDOKE, S. K., *Human Habitation Culture Environment Interface*. Printed by School of Planning and Architecture and Har-Anand Publications in association with Vikas Publishing House Pvt. Ltd., New Delhi, 1991.

CHOPRA, DEEPAK, *Creating Health*. Published by Houghton Mifflin Company, Boston, 1991.

CHOUDHURY, B., *Vegetables*. Published by National Book Trust of India, New Delhi, first edition 1967; reprinted 1992.

COWEN, D. V. *Flowering Trees and Shrubs in India*. Published by Thacker & Co. Ltd., Bombay, first edition 1950; revised edition 1984.

DALJEET, DR. *The Glory of Indian Miniatures*. Published by Mahindra Publications, Ghaziabad, 1988.

DASGUPTA, SURENDRANATH, *A History of Indian Philosophy*. Published by Motilal Banarasidass, New Delhi, 1975.

DASH, V. BHAGWAN, *Fundamentals of Ayurvedic Medicine*. Printed by Konark Publishers, Delhi, first edition 1978; revised edition 1989.

DASH, V. BHAGWAN and M. ACARYA MANFRED JUNIS, *A Handbook of Ayurveda*. Printed by Concept Publishing Co., New Delhi, first edition 1983; reprinted 1988.

DASTUR, J. F., *Medicinal Plants of India and Pakistan*. Published by D. B. Taraporevala Sons Pvt. Ltd., Bombay, 1962; reprinted 1988.

DASTUR, J. F., *Useful Plants of India and Pakistan*. Published by D. B. Taraporevala Sons Pvt. Ltd., Bombay, 1964.

DASTUR, J. F., *Everybody's Guide to Ayurvedic Medicine*. Published by D. B. Taraporevala Sons Pvt. Ltd., Bombay, first edition 1960; reprinted 1988.

ELWIN, VERRIER, *Tribal Myths of Orissa*. Published by Oxford University Press, Bombay, 1954.

FILLIOZAT, J., *The Classical Doctrine of Indian Medicine*. Printed by Munshiram Manohar Lal Publishers Pvt. Ltd., New Delhi, 1964.

GRIEVE, MRS. M., *A Modern Herbal*, vol. II. First published by Harcourt, Brace & Co., 1931; first Dover edition 1971; Index of Scientific Names compiled by M. Marshall, New York, 1982.

GRIFFITH, R. T. H., *The Hymns of the Rgveda*. Published by Motilal Banarasi Lal, New Delhi, 1976.

GUPTA, SHAKTI M. *Plants Myths and Traditions in India*. Published by Munshiram Manohar Lal Publishers Pvt. Ltd., New Delhi, 1991.

JOLLY, DR. JULIUS, *Indian Medicine*. Translated by C. G. Kashikar. Second revised edition printed by Munshiram Manohar Lal Publishers Pvt. Ltd., New Delhi, 1977.

KIRTIKAR K. R. and B. D. BASU, *Indian Medicinal Plants* 4 vols. text, 4 vols. illustrations. First published 1918; reprinted by B. S. Mahendra Pal Singh & Co., DehraDun, 1991.

KRISHNAMURTHY, K. H., *Traditional Family Medicine*. Published by Books for All, Delhi.

KURUP, DR. P. N. V. and DR. V. N.K. RAMADAS, and PRAJAPATI JOSHI, *Handbook of Medicinal Plants*. Published by Central Council for Research in Ayurveda and Siddha, New Delhi, 1979.

LAL, K. S., *History of the Khaljis*. Printed by Munshiram Manohar Lal Publishers Pvt. Ltd., New Delhi, 1980.

LATHAM, RONALD, translator, *Marco Polo, "The Travels."* Penguin Books, England, 1980.

LUST, JOHN B., *The Herb Book.* Published by Bantam Books, New York, 1974.

MAJUPURIA, T. C., *Religious and Useful Plants of Nepal and India.* Revised by D. P. Joshi. Second revised edition published by M. Gupta & Co., Gwalior, 1989.

McCANN, CHARLES, *Trees of India: A Popular Handbook.* Published by Periodical Expert Book Agency, Delhi, 1985.

MONIER-WILIAMS, SIR MONIER, *Sanskrit-English Dictionary.* First published by Oxford University Press, 1899. Reprinted by Motilal Banarasidass, New Delhi, 1990.

MUKHERJI, A. C., *Hindu Fasts and Feasts.* First edition printed in 1918; second edition published by Vintage Books, Gurgaon, 1989.

NADKARNI, DR. K. M., *Indian Materia Medica*, vols. I and II. Revised by K. Nadkarni. Published by Bombay Popular Prakashan, Bombay, first edition 1908; reprinted 1992.

NAG CHAUDHURI, B. D., editor, *New Technological Civilization and Indian Society.* Published by Indian Institute of Advanced Study, Simla, in association with Indus Publishing Company, New Delhi, 1990.

PANDEY, B. P. *Sacred Plants of India.* Published by Shree Publishing House, New Delhi, 1989.

PFLEIDERER, I., *The Life of Indian Plants.* Printed by Royal Publications, Delhi, 1990.

POLUNIN, OLEG and ADAM STAINTON, *Flowers of the Himalaya.* Published by Oxford University Press, New Delhi, first edition 1984; fifth edition 1989.

RAY, PRIYADARANJAN and HIRENDRA NATH GUPTA, *Charaka Samhita, A Scientific Synopsis.* Published by Indian National Science Academy, New Delhi, 1980.

ROGERS, ALEXANDER, *Tuzuk-i-Jahangiri (Memories of Jahangir).* Edited by Henry Beveridge. First published 1909–14; reprinted by Low Price Publications, Delhi, 1989.

ROHDE, ELEANOUR SINCLAIR, *The Old English Herbals.* Dover Publications, Inc., New York, 1971.

SARMA, SUDARSANA, *Plants in Yajurveda.* Published by K. S. Vidya Peetha, Tirupati, 1989.

SATYAVATI, DR. G. V., DR. K. ASHOK GUPTA, and NEERAJ TANDON, *Medicinal Plants of India*, vols. I and II. Published by Indian Council of Medical Research, New Delhi, 1987.

SENSARMA, P., *Plants in the Indian Puranas.* Published by B. Mitra Nayaprokash, Calcutta, 1989.

SHARMA, AYURVEDCHAKRAVARTY D. P., *Treatise on Thirty Important Baidyanath Ayurvedic Products.* Supervised by Dr. R. R. Pathak and R. B. Arora. Published by Shree Baidyanath Ayurved Bhawan Ltd., Patna, 1977.

SHARMA, P. V., *Dravyaguna-Vijnana*, vol. II. First printed 1978; ninth edition published by Chaukhambha Orientalia, Varanasi, 1987.

SIMONETTI, GUALTIEREO, *Guide to Herbs and Spices*. Published by Simon & Schuster, New York, 1974.

SINGH, KHUSHWANT and SUDDHASATTWA BASU, *Nature Watch*. Published by Lustre Press Pvt. Ltd., New Delhi, 1990.

SINHA, B. C., *Tree Worship in Ancient India*. Published by Books Today, New Delhi, 1979.

SPEAR, PERCIVAL, *A History of India*, vol. II. First published by Pelican Books, London, 1965; reprinted by Penguin Books, New Delhi, 1990.

THAPAR, ROMILA, *A History of India*, vol. I. First published by Pelican Books, London, 1966; reprinted by Penguin Books, New Delhi, 1990, 1992.

WATT, SIR GEORGE, *The Commercial Products of India*. Published by John Murray, London, 1908.

WELCH, S. C., *Imperial Mughal Painting*. Published by George Braziller, New York, 1978.

YULE, COL. HENRY and A. C. BURNELL, *Hobson-Jobson Glossary of Colloquial Anglo-Indian Words and Phrases, and of Kindred Terms, Etymological, Historical, Geographical and Discursive*. First published by John Murray, London, 1903. Fourth edition printed by Munshiram Manohar Lal Publishers Pvt. Ltd., New Delhi, 1984.

Index

Acknowledgments

I would like to thank Dr. V.N.K. Ramadas of the Central Council for Research in Ayurveda and Siddha, New Delhi, and Dr. T. N. Manjunath of the Voluntary Health Association of India, New Delhi, for their invaluable advice on the medicinal aspects of Ayurvedic plants, for their generosity in loaning me their published books and articles, and for allowing me access to their private collections of botanical photographs. I am greatly indebted to Pria Devi for her assistance in organizing my research material, and for locating many of the quotes from early Indian texts which I have used. My thanks to Dr. Jaweed Ashraf for loaning me his publications on environmental history, and to Drs. Romila Thapar, Jaweed Ashraf, and Tasleem Ahmed for their enlightening comments on the connections between Indian plants and Indian history. I am grateful to Dr. Daljeet of the National Museum, New Delhi, and Dr. Jyotindra Jain of the Crafts Museum, New Delhi, for their advice on Indian art. My thanks to Sheela Balaji and Aarti Aggarwala for sharing their knowledge on plant dyes; to Martand Singh and Mahijit Singh Jhala, for their support; to Pallavi Shah for her kind assistance; to Kunal Singh Rathore for his enthusiastic research; to Chandra Mohan for collating and typing research material; to R. K. Dutta Gupta for photographing botanical paintings; to Pankaj Jain for locating so many obscure research texts. I am grateful to my editor, Jacqueline Kennedy Onassis, for her support and encouragement. Finally, my thanks to my sister, Gita Mehta, without whom I could not have completed this book.

ABOUT THE AUTHOR

NAVEEN PATNAIK is a founding member of the Indian National Trust for Art and Cultural Heritage. He has published two previous books: *A Second Paradise: Indian Courtly Life 1590–1947*, and *A Desert Kingdom: The Rajputs of Bikaner*. He has written articles for cultural and environmental publications, and lives in New Delhi, India.